DON'T SIT IN THE DRAFT

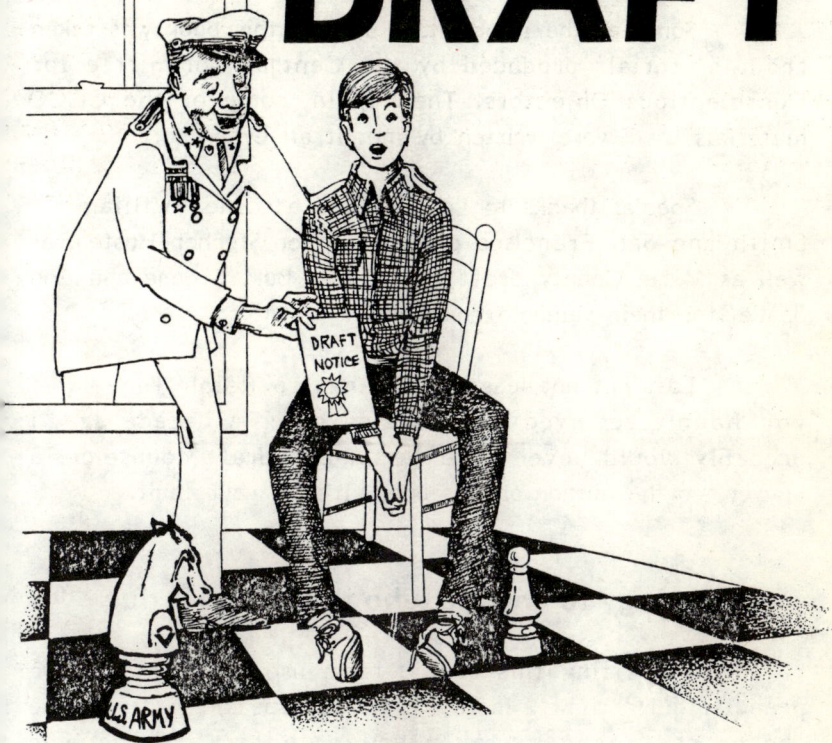

by
R. Charles Johnson
attorney

Editor: Charles E. Sherman

NOLO PRESS

P.O. Box 544, Occidental, CA 95465

Dedication

dedicated to

millions of young men

and to those who care about them

Acknowledgments

Some of the information used in this book was taken from materials produced by the Central Committee for Conscientious Objectors. Then again, some of the CCCO materials used were written by me. It all evens out.

Special thanks to Los Angeles attorney William G. Smith and San Francisco draft counselor Stephen Huston, as well as Marin County draft counselors Burt Greene and Ann Spake, for their valuable comments.

Last but not least, my thanks to Ralph Teevan. If you hadn't received an induction order a decade ago, I probably would never have become a draft counselor, a lawyer, or the author of this book. It's all your fault.

Apology to anyone who thinks one is due

In writing this book I have used the masculine pronoun quite a bit. In my everyday speaking I try to use "he or she" as much as possible, but it can become distracting and annoying in the printed form. Also, at present the draft laws apply only to men, and no one can second-guess what the US Supreme Court is going to do about that. Since only men are subject to the draft, use of the masculine pronoun seems appropriate.

ISBN 0-917316-32-0

10/81

READ ALL ABOUT IT!

• NOLO UPDATE SERVICE •

The material in this book is up to date at the time of printing, but the rules and regulations can change, and from time to time they do. For this reason, you should make sure you have the most recent edition of this book. But why take chances? If you mail us the coupon below, together with a **stamped, self-addressed envelope**, we will notify you if any important changes take place in the next year.

HANDY COUPON

TABLE OF CONTENTS

PART ONE: THE OPENING GAME
★ REGISTRATION ★

FOREWORD..9

1. HOW THE DRAFT SYSTEM WORKS..................15
   The draft system for the 80's
   The urgent need to be prepared

2. WINING & LOSING IN THE DRAFT LOTTERY.........23
   Order of call
   Extended priority
   First priority
   Second priority

3. ENLISTING TO BEAT THE DRAFT....................35
   Reserves, National Guard & Coast Guard
   Enlistment promises and contracts
   Tips for enlistees

4. REGISTRATION AND RESISTANCE...................41
   Leave the country?
   Non-registration
   Non-registration is not an easy way out
   Going underground
   If caught
   Registration procedure
   Resistance after registration

PART TWO: THE MIDDLE GAME
★ CLASSIFICATION ★

5. CLASSIFICATION, EXEMPTION AND DEFERMENT......59

6. CONSCIENTIOUS OBJECTION.......................65
   1-A-O and 1-O conscientious objection
   Who qualifies?
   The six questions
   When to file
   Alternate service work
   Some points for 1-Os to consider

7. DEPENDENCY DEFERMENTS........................ 81
      Financial dependency
      Physical dependency
      Emotional dependency
      Filing for 3-A

8. SURVIVING SONS.................................89
      Sole surviving son
      Surviving sons
      General provisions

9. MINISTERS AND MINISTERIAL STUDENTS............. 93
      Ministers
      Theology students

10. MEDICAL SPECIALISTS AND MEDICAL STUDENTS....97
      Order of call
      Deferment or exemption
      Sliding by a special call
      Medical students

11. HOW TO DEAL WITH
    A DISAGREEABLE CLASSIFICATION 105
      The appeal process
      Why you should appeal
      How to appeal
      Communicating with the SS

★ PART THREE: THE END GAMES ★

APPEALS, 4-F, REFUSING INDUCTION, COURT

12. THE LOCAL BOARD PERSONAL APPEARANCE 115
      Witnesses
      Why appeal?
      Some guidelines
      Courtesy interviews
      Playing draftboard
      At the personal appearance
      More paperwork
      Notification of results

13. THE STATE APPEAL AND BEYOND.................135
      Checking the file
      Preparing the file
      The state appeal
      If denied again

14. THE MEDICAL EXAMINATION:
    IF YOU DON'T PASS IT YOU'RE OUT...............145
      The physical fitness standards
      Documentation
      What to do with the report
      The physical exam
      Re-examination
      Being gay
      Some unusual cases
      Conclusion

15. INDUCTION: WHAT TO DO WHEN YOU'RE CALLED 165
      Accepting induction
      Requesting immediate discharge
      Posponement or cancellation
      Leaving the country
      Refusing induction
      What happens after refusal
      Looking for a lawyer

16. DRAFT CASES IN COURT 183
      Procedural errors
      Ungranted classification
      Constitutionality
      Other lines of defense
      Sentencing practices

APPENDIXES

A. ALIENS AND THE DRAFT..........................199
B. COUNSELING AGENCIES   207
C. MEDICAL STANDARDS   208
D. FOOTNOTES   231

PART ONE: THE OPENING GAME

REGISTRATION

FOREWORD!

YOU **CAN** BEAT THE DRAFT. I know, because I helped hundreds of people do it during the Vietnam war. All it takes is access to accurate information about the draft law, the perserverance to keep working at it, the assistance of a good draft counselor, and (sometimes) a little luck.

This book contains the highlights of information and advice that I developed in over 10 years of draft counseling and lawyering. This book is not a substitute for good draft counseling. Rather, the purpose is to give you enough information about the draft and your alternatives to allow you to make intelligent decisions. With good information a man can get a lot more help from his draft counselor, since they can get down to real business instead of spending a lot of time discussing basic things.

It is my hope that the readers of this book will be well served by it. Comments or criticisms from readers are always appreciated.

Draft counselors & lawyers

There are many misconceptions about draft counseling. Some people feel that draft counselors can keep men from being drafted, while others may feel that counseling is useless. Many feel that it is every man's duty to "serve his country," and that draft counselors encourage people to be unpatriotic or to break the law. Still others feel that draft counselors can give out draft deferments or exemptions.

9

The purpose of draft counseling is to inform people of their rights and obligations under the draft law, and to help people to make decisions that are right for them. Once a man has made his decision, a counselor can help him deal with the bureaucracy of the Selective Service System. A lot of people seem to think that draft counselors can hand them a list of "ways to get out." Not only would that be impossible to do, it would also completely defeat the purpose of counseling. It is not a counselor's job to make decisions for other people, or to map out their lives for them. The purpose of counseling is to advise people of the probable consequences of their intended actions, and to help them find a course of action which will best serve their individual needs.

Each of us is an individual human being, and has the right to make his own decisions and to control his own life. No one has the right to make another person's decisions for him. Of course, there are many people who claim to have that right, such as schools, parents, friends, governments, and so on. But we are all free to decide for ourselves, and **must** decide for ourselves if we are to keep that freedom. For a draft counselor to be added to the list of people willing to control other peoples' lives would be a gross mistake.

A good counselor will make sure you are aware of all possible alternatives and probable consequences. He or she will try to learn everything possible about your personal feelings, politics and philosophy, and help you decide for yourself what you want to do. The two of you will work together toward goals **you** choose. A counselor should encourage you to take responsibility for your own life.

You **must** decide as early as possible what you want to do about the draft. The longer you wait to decide, the fewer alternatives you have left. If you don't ever decide, it may suddenly be too late. Then the government will decide for you . . . their way.

Will you go into the military if ordered? Are you going to work within the system for a deferment or exemption? Are you going to refuse to cooperate with the system? If so, at what point? Will you refuse to register for the draft? Will you refuse induction if ordered? Are you willing to go to jail or leave the country rather than cooperate with the system? These are difficult decisions to make, but a good counselor can tell you what you can expect in each case, as well as help you decide what will best serve your needs and desires, both now and in the future.

If a you already know what you want to do (perhaps as a result of reading this book) a counselor can be even more help. A counselor can help you go after the deferment or exemption you want with greatly improved chances of getting it, or set up your draft resistance case with the least chance of ending up in prison. If you want to leave the country, a counselor may be able to help you do so legally, and in a way that may permit you to come back to the United States later without facing a trial.

These things and more can be done, but it takes a lot of will-power, knowledge, and just plain hard work. Don't expect it to be easy, because it isn't. But then again, going into the military is no picnic, either.

Most big cities are setting up draft counseling centers, and larger cities may have more than one. These centers are usually staffed by non-lawyer draft counselors, although many centers have lawyers who volunteer time as well. With a few exceptions, draft counseling is a free service. Naturally, most counseling centers could put a donation to very good use. Funding for draft counseling is usually difficult to get, and even a dollar or two would be a big help in paying office rent or phone bills.

In addition to these "lay counselors," there are also lawyers who specialize in draft law cases. Draft law is not learned in law school, so being a lawyer, even a good criminal defense lawyer, does not indicate an ability to handle draft cases. Many of the tactics which lawyers use in handling other administrative agency cases, or other kinds of criminal defense cases, simply will not work in a draft case. By the same token, many of the most useful tactics and defenses in draft cases exist nowhere else in the law. The Selective Service System is a bureaucracy with its own extensive set of rules and regulations. The area of draft law is highly specialized, and only someone intimately familiar with its intricacies is going to be able to adequately handle a draft case. Naturally, a private lawyer who handles draft cases is not going to take cases for free.

Dealing with the draft occurs on two levels: administrative and judicial. The administrative end involves dealing with the bureaucracy of the system - registration, applying for deferments or exemptions, and so on. For those functions either a lay counselor or a lawyer can be helpful. The judicial level involves court actions, such as possible prosecution for violating the draft law, suing the system, and so on, and in such cases, a lawyer is needed.

Whether to work with a counselor or a lawyer must be an individual decision. Some draft counselors are highly skilled and extremely knowledgable, while others aren't. Some will be sensitive to a man's needs, while others may seem to use people for their own ends. By the same token, some lawyers have vast experience in draft law, while others know less than many draft counselors. The important thing is to get the best counseling available, and to find someone you can trust and feel confident working with. Whether that means a counselor or a lawyer depends on you and your circumstances - shop around.

How to spot good counseling

There are several points to watch for in looking for a counselor. Before offering advice, a good counselor will ask many questions, either in the form of a printed questionnaire, or through discussion, or both. He will try to find out what you want to do and why. He will make sure that you are fully aware of all the alternatives open to you, and will be willing to discuss those choices and their probable consequences. He will ask about your beliefs and values and try to understand them without imposing his own. Beware of a counselor who tells people "how to get out" or who "guarantees" that he can get men out of the draft. He may be a knowledgable counselor, but he also may be more interested in his own point of view than in yours. And, after all, it is your life and your decisions that are being discussed.

By the way, "he" may be "she," as some of the best counselors are women, but it seemed awkward to keep saying "he or she" over and over again. Please forgive me, ladies.

No draft counselor or lawyer knows the answer to every question. A good counselor never guesses. If he doesn't know the answer to a question, he will say so. If the information is important to you, the counselor will know where to find the answer, and will help you find it.

Since people and the law are constantly changing, the information a counselor gives one man may not be valid for others, and may not even be valid for anyone several months later. A good counselor will encourage you to stay in touch. Counseling is rarely a one-shot affair. It may take weeks, months or even years for a person to make decisions and act on them. A counselor will offer moral support through the rough times, as well as help you re-evaluate your position whenever you feel the need.

The way to spot a good draft lawyer is basically the same as looking for a good counselor. As with counselors, be wary of any lawyer who "guarantees" that he can keep you from being drafted. No one can guarantee any such thing, and anyone who claims to be able to do so is not being truthful. Even in seemingly clear-cut cases, things can go wrong and the individual can end up being drafted.

Another common area for caution is the lawyer who boasts of his "win record" being 100%, or some other high figure. While it may seem impressive at first, it might only mean that this lawyer refuses to take any difficult cases. As a fellow lawyer, I have more respect for a lawyer with a lower "win record" who takes really tough cases and still manages to pull some off. Best of all, I prefer a lawyer who doesn't bother to keep track of percentages.

People who decide to work with a lawyer are going to have to be prepared to pay legal fees. Fees vary from place to place, and from lawyer to lawyer. Some lawyers charge a flat fee, while others charge an hourly rate. A few phone calls in your community should give you a good idea of what the "average" legal fees are like.

One last word of caution - you are better off finding one counselor or lawyer you feel comfortable with and sticking with that person. One of the easiest ways I know of for you to screw up your case is to take bits and pieces of advice from several counselors. We all work a little differently, and shopping around for the easiest answers may be the kiss of death.

If you need help finding a draft counselor or lawyer near you, get in touch with one of the organizations listed in the back of this book, and they will help you. A national list grows and changes too frequently to be printed here, as it would almost immediately become outdated. However, the organizations listed in Appendix B are permanent and in touch with draft counseling across the nation.

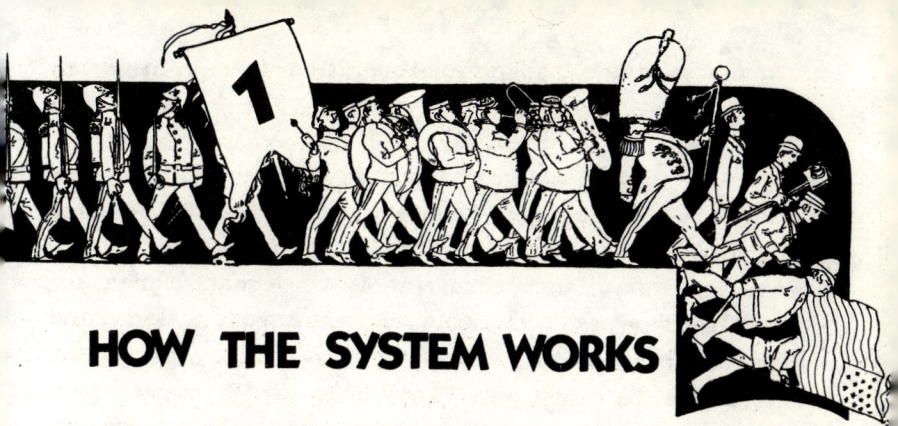

HOW THE SYSTEM WORKS

It is important to understand how the system works in order to anticipate what it will do to you, and to be able to get what you want from it. As my grandfather used to tell me, "The more you know about the rules of a game, the luckier you are at it."

The Selective Service System as it existed during the Vietnam era was a cumbersome, bumbling bureaucracy. Draft registrants who knew how the system operated were often able to hog-tie it in its own red tape and avoid being drafted. As a result, the system designed for use in the eighties has been streamlined in many respects. Many changes are still to come, but we do have a very good idea of how the new system will work.

The Selective Service System exists because of the Military Selective Service Act[1] - the draft law. That law has been on the books continuously since 1948 and is in effect right now. It authorizes the Selective Service System to exist, and authorizes the President to register for the draft, when and as he pleases, all men between the ages of eighteen and twenty-six. He also has the authority **right now** to classify those men, order them for physical examinations, and do everything except actually order them to be inducted into the military. The Congressional debate during the summer of 1980 was **not** over the President's authority to register men. He already had that authority. It was only over the budget appropriation to pay for draft registration.

At present, only men born in 1960 and later years are required to register. No one is being classified, ordered for a physical examination, or otherwise processed,[2] but the possibility of those steps occurring is very real. Under our streamlined system, it could all begin very swiftly and without much warning.

The System exists on three levels: local, regional and national. At present, the national level is made up of a handful of government employees (many of them military reserve officers) who write regulations, answer questions from the government and the public, and maintain the computers which hold information about men who have been registered for the draft.

There are five regional Selective Service offices, each covering several states. At present their only job is to be prepared for a resumption of inductions, as well as to supervise the registration process in their area.

The draft system for the 80's

There is no local level at present, although it will quickly be re-established in the future if inductions begin. The System at the local level will exist in two forms. There will be over four hundred "area offices," and there will also be a network of "draft boards," more properly called Selective Service local boards. The local board is a group of three to five local residents who volunteer to serve on the board.[3] They are not paid, but serve for free. Each local board covers a certain area, at least one to each county. Some counties have only one local board, while some large cities may have dozens of local boards.[4] To serve on a local board a person must be between the ages of eighteen and sixty-five, must live in the area which the board covers, and must be recommended by the Governor of the state and approved by the President of the United States.

Draft registrants will not be assigned to a local board until drafting begins. Even then not all registrants will be assigned to a local board. Men who receive an induction order and comply with it will never be assigned to a local board. Men who request deferment or exemption from the draft will have their claim reviewed by an area office. In cases where the deferment or exemption claim does not require the system to make a judgment or exercise its discretion (such as a claim for exemption as a veteran) the area office may simply grant the requested classification. In cases where discretion is involved, such as claims for conscientious objector status, the matter will be sent to a local board for processing, and the man making the claim will be assigned to that local board. However, local board power is not all-encompassing.

On questions of whether or not to grant deferments or exemptions from the draft, a denial by a local board can be reviewed by an Appeal Board at the state level.[5] If denied there, it may be possible to get further consideration from a national Appeal Board.[6] This process is discussed more fully in Chapters 12 and 13.

Outside the Selective Service System, but working hand-in-glove with it, is the Army-run Armed Forces Examining and Entrance Stations (AFEES). These stations administer physical exams to all people entering the military, both those who enlist and those who are drafted.[7] Only the AFEES can find someone physically unfit for induction.[8] More information about physical exemptions appears in Chapter 14.

Much is still unclear about how the draft system will work this time around. We know how the registration system works, we know how the system is structured, we

know the legal penalties for violations of the law, and we know that certain deferments and exemptions will be available. Deferments and exemptions are legal ways to avoid being drafted. Some get you off the hook for a while, some for good.

What we don't know for sure are the exact procedures which will be followed. For instance, we know there will be a "lottery" system used to decide the order in which people will be drafted. But it is unclear whether only one lottery drawing will be held for all men registered at the time inductions begin, or whether, for instance, separate drawings will be held for men born in 1960, 1961, and so on. (See Chapter 2.) We know there will be a right to appeal a local board decision denying a deferment, but don't know how long a man will have to appeal - present regulations say fifteen days,[9] but that could be changed at any time. Considering the efficiency of our postal system lately, it had better be extended.

Some of the procedures are very much up in the air since the regulations say one thing and the President's Report to Congress says another. Another report, the Emergency Military Manpower Procurement System (EMMPS) Manual, proposes several changes to existing Selective Service regulations and procedures. This book assumes that while many of the procedures used during the Vietnam draft will remain the same, the proposals in the President's Report and the EMMPS Manual will be implemented. But the law can change overnight. Nothing here should be relied upon in dealing with the system without first checking with a lawyer or counselor who understands draft law to make sure that it is still valid. Future editions of this book will be updated with changes to keep current with the latest known laws and procedures. If you cut out the "Update Service" coupon at the front of this book, and mail it to us with a stamped, self-addressed envelope, we will notify you if important changes take place.

The President's Report to Congress in February, 1980, outlines a plan for drafting people which drastically streamlines the system used during Vietnam.[10] The President is currently authorized to order not only registration, but lottery drawings, physical examinations and local board supervised classification as well. However, he has said that he will not order more than registration until the government decides to resume inductions.[11] This announcement is in line with the mobilization standards set out in the EMMPS Manual.

For inductions to resume, Congress would first have to pass a bill authorizing inductions (and presumably appropriating funds as well).[12] That could occur after prolonged debate, or it could happen in one day, with no warning or debate. The **same** day Congress authorizes inductions, lottery drawings will be held to determine the order in which men will be drafted. That **same day** those receiving low lottery numbers will automatically be sent orders to report for induction as soon as ten days later.

Claims for deferment or exemption from the draft will have to be made within that ten day period or forever given up.

Local boards will be set up to hear deferment or exemption claims. Physical examinations at AFEES will be given on a massive scale, estimated in the report at 7,000 per day, six days per week. They are given on the day you report for induction. Those who are found physically qualified and have not requested a deferment or exemption will be inducted into the military that day.

The first draftees will be in uniform within thirteen days after a Congressional decision to begin drafting. The report anticipates inducting up to 100,000 men within the first 28 days after the Congressional decision to draft, and up to 650,000 within the first six months.

20

Your classification will determine whether or not you are subject to being drafted.[13] The Selective Service System uses twenty-two classifications to categorize men subject to the draft. If you are classified into some of these categories, your induction will be postponed. This is called a "deferment." People in some of the other classifications are not subject to draft at all. This is called "exemption."

To begin with, you will be presumed to be 1-A eligible for draft, but if you act fast you can apply for reclassification to another category which will defer or exempt you from the draft. Part Two is devoted to explaining how to understand and use the rules on classification to your best advantage.

The urgent need to be prepared

When induction notices first go out, claims for deferment or exemption will have to be made within 10 days of the date the notices were mailed or forever given up.

Anyone wishing to obtain a draft deferment or exemption cannot afford to delay. With only days in which to request deferment or exemption, it is absolutely essential that claims be prepared well ahead of time. Once inductions begin, draft counselors will be swamped and unable to give individual attention to very many men, if any. Civilian doctors willing to document existing grounds for medical exemption will be able to see only a very few of those needing their services. The release of medical records alone could take far longer than ten days. The documentation needed for other deferment or exemption claims may not be available on such short notice. If you wait until it hits the fan, it may be too late to duck.

During Vietnam most people ordered for induction were put into the Army, but thousands ended up in the Marine Corps. In either event, most draftees ended up in combat units on the front lines in Vietnam. Is that something you are willing to do? If you don't make your decision, the government will make it for you.

There are many alternatives available to you and many ways you can deal with the draft. These are all discussed in the pages below, but the success of most plans depends upon getting an early start on your preparation and planning. It is never too late to start planning, but it is never too early, either. An early start on a good plan gives you an excellent chance of getting your way with the system. That's what the rest of this book is about.

WINNING AND LOSING
IN THE DRAFT LOTTERY

The United States has a national lottery. It is only drawn occasionally, but media coverage is much bigger that way. It doesn't cost any money to participate - you just need to have been born in the right year. There are tens of thousands of potential winners, and each winner will receive a guaranteed full-time job for two years. Many winners in the past have received an all-expense-paid vacation in a foreign country. Tens of thousands of past lucky winners have even had their burial costs paid. The U.S. lottery seems somewhat warped, though, because if you win, you lose; if you lose, you win.

The mechanics of a draft lottery drawing are simple enough. Each date of the calandar year (January 1 through December 31) is written down, placed in a separate plastic capsule, and tossed into a bucket. Another bucket holds capsules containing the numbers 1 through 365 (or 366 if a leap year is involved). Capsules are drawn from each bucket, one at a time, and matched up, so each date of the year is assigned a number. There is no logical order to the numbers assigned. Each date of the year has an equal chance of getting lottery number 1, or number 365, or any number in between.

The dates of the year represent the birth dates of draft registrants. Everyone subject to the lottery who is born on the same date gets the same lottery number. The lottery numbers themselves indicate the order in which people could be drafted: number one will be the first to go, then number two, and so on.

There is no way to change a lottery number once it has been assigned.[1] The number assigned to you is based upon the date the SS records show as your date of birth at the time the lottery drawing is held. Even if the date they have on file is wrong - if you gave the wrong date when you registered, or if someone messed up while feeding the computer - once your lottery number has been assigned you cannot have it changed.

During the Vietnam draft, lottery numbers were assigned in two slightly different ways. When the lottery system was begun in 1969, a single lottery drawing was held to assign numbers to all registrants who were then between the ages of nineteen and twenty-five. No matter where in that age-group a man was, if he was born on January 15 he received lottery number 17, and so on. In later years new drawings were held to assign numbers to registrants who turned nineteen years old during the year of the drawing. For instance, a lottery drawing was held during 1970 to assign lottery numbers to people born in 1951, who would turn nineteen that year. In this way a lottery number depended not only upon a man's date of birth, but his year of birth as well, since a given date might receive a low lottery number one year and a high lottery number the next year.

Under the system used in the early seventies, no matter what a man's lottery number, he could not be drafted until the calendar year during which he would turn twenty. For example, a person born in December, 1962, could be drafted in January, 1982, even though he would not actually turn twenty until the end of that year. Draft liability is based on the calendar year of your birth, not the actual date.

The "calendar year" concept also creates another misconception. The law currently says that the calendar year during which you turn twenty is the **earliest** that you can be drafted.[2] However, merely getting through that year without actually being inducted into the military does not mean that you are safe. For instance, if drafting were to begin in 1982, it is possible that one lottery drawing could be held for all men born in 1960 through 1962, similar to the 1969 drawing. All men with low lottery numbers could be called, regardless of whether they turned twenty in 1980, 1981 or 1982.

By the same token, gaining a deferment or exemption for the year in which a man turns twenty may not end his liability either. Let's say that a man born in 1962 gets lottery number 6. Drafting begins in 1982 (the calendar year in which he turns twenty) and lottery numbers 1 through 200 are called. Our man receivs an induction order in January, since the call for that month is for lottery number 1 through 25 to be inducted. But he immediately sends his area office information saying that he is enrolled in a divinity school, and so receivs a 2-D deferment throughout 1982. In 1983, he decides to drop out of divinity school and become a garbage collector. He feels safe about the draft, since he made it through the year in which he turned twenty without being inducted. But he is not safe! When his deferment ends he will be put into the Extended Priority Selection Group for 1983 and drafted ahead of men turning twenty that year. And he will still have lottery number 6, even though men turning twenty during 1983 who share his day and month of birth will probably get a higher number in a later drawing. In other words, once a man gets a lottery number he is stuck with it. And being deferred during the year in which a man turns twenty may only delay things, since he may be put back into the draft pool if he later loses his deferment before he turns twenty-six.

Some time after the lottery drawing is held, a "ceiling number" may be set by the SS for that lottery pool.

For instance, in July 1972 a "ceiling number" of 100 was set for the lottery pool drawn February 2, 1972. The ceiling number is the highest lottery number that the SS expects to draft out of that pool. There is no requirement that a ceiling number be set, and if the SS expects to draft large numbers of people it is unlikely that one will be set. For instance, if the SS intended to issue draft calls such as those issued during the Vietnam and Korean wars, it is possible that all members of the First Priority Group will be called, and therefore no ceiling number will be set. A discussion of Priority Groups appears below.

If a ceiling number is set, anyone whose lottery number is higher than the ceiling number set for his lottery pool will most likely be classified 1-H and not be drafted, unless there were an unexpected draft increase, such as a declaration of war or national emergency. The ceiling number is **not** a guarantee that those with higher numbers won't be drafted, but once the number is set it is very unlikely that the SS will later raise it unless a national mobilization occurred. People with lottery numbers equal to or lower than the ceiling number will, of course, be processed for induction.

Order of call

In order to understand the system, we first have to get rid of the idea that **only** lottery numbers determine whether or not a person will be inducted. In actuality, lottery numbers play only a part in the draft system. The real question is: who is available for induction and who in that group is eligible?

The lottery system comes into play only after the other administrative processes have determined who is **available** to be drafted. Only when a person is considered fully available and eligible for induction does the lottery system take on full meaning. Of those people found to be eligible and available, the lottery numbers will help to select those who will be inducted, and in what order they will be called.

There is an over-all system known as the "Order of Call" which affects those people who are available to be drafted. The lottery is part of the Order of Call, but only a part. In order to understand the meaning of the lottery system, we should also understand the Order of Call.

The Order of Call is a method of ranking people who are available to be drafted by putting people into various "priority groups" for being drafted. People in the highest priority group have the highest likelihood of being drafted, and will be called first whenever there is a draft call. People in the lower priority groups have less chance of being drafted, and will be drafted last, if ever. When drafting people, the SS **must** follow the Order of Call. No one can be called from a given priority group until **all** people in higher priority groups have been called.[3]

A chart of the Order of Call appears below, listed from top to bottom in order of priority, along with a short explanation of what each priority group means.

Volunteer: People between the ages of seventeen and twenty-five who volunteer to be drafted will be called before anyone else. The orders will be sent in the order in which people volunteered, regardless of age or lottery number.

Extended Priority: These are people who would have been inducted during the previous year, but for some reason were not. This includes people who were deferred or otherwise found temporarily unavailable during the previous year. Being put in this group effectively gives a person a lottery number lower than number one, since members of the Extended Priority Group will be called before lottery number one in the First Priority Group.

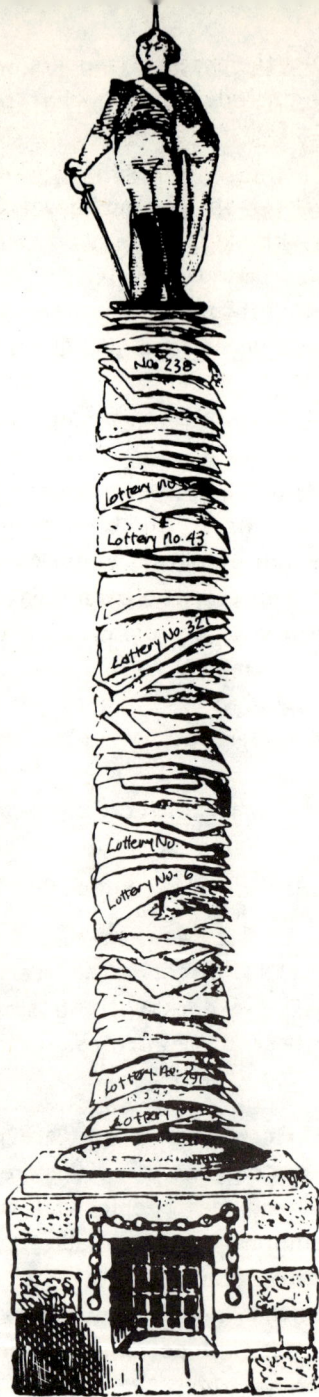

First Priority: This is the group for people who are eligible for the first time to be drafted. If drafting starts, this group may consist of people who will turn twenty during that year, or it may include all registrants who will turn twenty **or older** (up to age twenty-six) that year. In later years of drafting it will be composed of men who turn twenty during that year. People can be called from the First Priority Group **only** in lottery number order, starting with number one and progressing toward number 365 or 366.

Second Priority: People who were in the Fist Priority Group during the previous year, but whose lottery numbers were not reached in First Priority during that year.

Third Priority: People who were in the First Priority Group two years previously, but whose lottery numbers were not reached in First Priority during that year, or in the Second Priority during the next year.

Lower Priority Groups: There are other priority groups for people who are not yet old enough to enter the First Priority Group or who are over age twenty-six.

It is unlikely that drafting would occur out of any priority group lower than First Priority unless draft calls reached the level of the calls during the Vietnam or Korean wars.

Each year after drafting begins, a new First Priority Group will enter the Order of Call, since a new year-group of people will be turning twenty that year. To make room for them, the previous year's First Priority Group will be divided into two categories on January first. People whose lottery numbers were not reached during the previous year will be placed in the Second Priority Group, and all lower priority groups will move down one notch. For instance, the 1983 Second Priority Group will become the 1984 Third Priority Group on January 1, 1984, and so on. People in the

29

First Priority Group whose lottery numbers **were** reached during the year, but for some reason were not inducted, will be placed into the following year's Extended Priority Group.

Lottery numbers can be thought of as a more detailed order of call within the Order of Call. People who are in a particular priority group **must** be called in sequence by lottery number. In other words, just as it would be illegal to call people from the Second Priority Group without first reaching all lottery numbers in the higher priority groups, so too would it be illegal to call lottery number fifty from a priority group until everyone in that priority group with lottery numbers one through forty-nine had already been called.

Being called does not necessarily mean being inducted. For example, let's say that a local board is ordered to induct all people with lottery numbers one through fifty: they could have twenty people in the First Priority Group with those lottery numbers, and yet not actually induct anyone. Let's say that of those twenty people, twelve of them are found medically disqualified and given 4-F exemptions. Four others are currently divinity students, gaining 2-D student deferments. Two have been granted hardship deferments (3-A). The remaining two are appealing a local board denial of their claims for conscientious objector status. Since only those people who are both available **and eligible** can be inducted, no one from that local board can be inducted since they are either deferred, exempted, or using their appeal rights.

In the next sections, we will take a closer look at the three highest priority groups, the Extended, First and Second Priority Groups. We will ignore the Volunteer Group, since it needs no explanation other than to point out that it is comprised of people who volunteer for induction, which is not the same as enlisting in the military.

Etended priority

The Extended Priority Group is the first to be called whenever a non-volunteer draft call is made. There is only one way to get into Extended Priority: to have your lottery number reached during your year in First Priority. There are three ways to be removed from Extended Priority, but since one of those ways is to be inducted, we will discuss only the two escapes that may interest you.

The first way you get out of Extended Priority is if there are no draft calls during your first year in the Extended Priority Group.[4]

Let's say that Scott Sherwood was born in 1963. Drafting begins in 1983, and Scott is assigned lottery number 6. He managed to avoid being inducted during 1983, but his lottery number is reached during the January, 1983, draft call. Since his lottery number is reached during the year in which he is a member of the First Priority Group (the calendar year in which he turns twenty) he goes into the Extended Priority Group on January 1, 1984.[5]

Luckily for Scott, the draft is allowed to lapse on January 1, 1984, and there are no draft calls through December 31, 1984. Since on December 31 Scott has been a member of the Extended Priority Group for his entire first year of Extended Priority liability, and no draft calls have been sent out that year, Scott must be put into the Second Priority Group on January 1, 1985.

Had there been any draft call during 1984 Scott would most certainly have been called, since Extended Priority is the first group called upon, and his lottery number of 6 is extremely low. Even if Scott had not been actually inducted during 1984 (such as if he maintained a deferment throughout his entire first year in Extended Priority) he would still have been carried over into the 1985

Extended Priority Group, and so on until he was either inducted or turned twenty-six. You can see that unless drafting is allowed to lapse so that there are no draft calls for an entire year, this is not a very realistic way to get out of the Extended Priority Group.

The second way to "escape" the Extended Priority Group is to turn twenty-six years old. The problem, of course, is being able to stay out that long. About the only way to do that is to have a classification **other** than 1-A, 1-A-O, or 1-O; in other words, to have a deferment or exemption. The problem with this method is that the escape lasts only as long as the deferment or exemption. Should you lose your deferment or exemption you would be placed back into the Extended Priority Group. The trick to escaping in this manner is to stay deferred until age twenty-six. Immediately upon a man's twenty-sixth birthday, no matter when in the year it falls, he must be placed in the lower priority group for men over age twenty-five.[6] Classification, deferments and exemptions are discussed in great detail in Chapter 5.

First priority

After everyone in the Extended Priority Group has been called, the next group to be called upon is the First Priority Group. In practice, there has never been a draft call upon the Extended Priority Group alone. Rather, the January draft call is usually for everyone in Extended Priority and the first several lottery numbers from First Priority.

When inductions first begin there will be no Extended Priority Group, and everyone eligible to be called will be placed in the First Priority Group. First Priority is always the largest group, and includes everyone who is eligible for the first time during that year. Under present regulations the First Priority Group is to be composed of men who turn twenty during that year. But during the first year of inductions that regulation may be changed to define First Priority as all registrants who turn twenty **or older** that year.

It may be that not everyone from a First Priority Group will be called. In such cases the SS has in the past set a "ceiling number" reflecting the highest lottery number expected to be called from First Priority, and has assigned 1-H classifications to everyone whose lottery number was not expected to be reached. The ceiling number applies only to men in First Priority, and not the other priority groups. However, if there were large induction calls, such as was the case during the Vietnam war, it could be that everyone from First Priority would be called.

As mentioned earlier, no one can stay in the First Priority Group for more than one calendar year. At the end of the year a member of First priority is either placed into the Extended Priority Group (if his lottery number was reached during the year)[7] or into the Second Priority Group (if his lottery number was **not** reached during the year).[8]

One often hears street rumors that a person is only eligible to be drafted for one year. That is true **only** if your lottery number is not reached during the year that you are a member of the First Priority Group. If your number is reached, you will go into the Extended Priority Group the following year, and could remain there for as long as six years (until age twenty-six) or until otherwise removed from the Extended Priority Group.

There are other technicalities involved in determining who is or is not a member of the First Priority Group, and anyone who has any question about it should discuss the situation with a draft counselor or lawyer who understands the Order of Call.

Second priority

The Second Priority Group has in the past been the promised land for draft avoiders. Since people in the Second Priority Group can be called only if everyone in First Priority has been reached first, and since it seems unlikely that all of the First Priority Group will be called during any year (except in cases of massive mobilization), once a person makes it into the Second Priority Group, he breathes a sigh of relief.

There has never been a call out of the Second Priority Group. However, it is possible that the combination of a declining birth rate and a massive draft call could result in people from Second Priority being called. The relief of making it into the Second Priority Group is increased by the fact that each year moves you further away from the First Priority Group.[9] For instance, people in the Second Priority Group for 1982 will be in the Third Priority Group for 1983, the Fourth Priority Group for 1984, and so on until they turn age twenty-six.

If there is to be a draft call out of the Second Priority Group, it will have to be in lottery number order, and no one from the Third Priority Group can be called until all lottery numbers in the Second Priority Group have first been reached.

Actually, the lottery system and the Order of Call are more complex than this explanation. It became so complex during the Vietnam war that local boards were continually messing up and placing people in the wrong priority group. Despite SS attempts to simplify the system, there will no doubt be numerous errors made in the future. Anyone having any questions regarding his lottery number or his priority should check carefully with a counselor or lawyer who is experienced in the technicalities of this area of draft law.

ENLISTING TO BEAT THE DRAFT

People sometimes consider the possibility of enlisting in the military as an alternative to being drafted. Joining the military in order to keep from being drafted into the military makes about as much sense as destroying a village in order to save it. If you don't want to go into the military, why consider it as an option? Being drafted is not inevitable, and no one should enlist simply because he feels pressured by the draft.

Some men enlist, thinking they can get a better deal than if they are drafted. This is what recruiters would like you to think, but it is not necessarily true. If you do decide to enlist in the military the local recruiters will no doubt be very happy to help you, but before you do it a few words of caution are in order.

Reserves, National Guard & Coast Guard

During the Vietnam war it became common for people to enlist in a branch of the military reserves to avoid being drafted and sent to Vietnam. While it worked then, people considering the reserves today should give it some deep thought. When the United States became involved in Southeast Asia in the mid-sixties, the military wanted to send thousands of troops overseas immediately. Draft calls shot up, but draftees take several months to train. In order to quickly meet the rising demand for trained personnel, tens of thousands of military reservists were called to active duty and many were sent to Vietnam. It was only later in the war that active duty strength was high enough to meet military manpower requirements, and the reserves became known as an outfit of weekend soldiers.

If the United States becomes involved in another war there is every reason to believe that a similar pattern will occur, and that reservists will be called to active duty in large numbers early in the war. If you join a reserve unit now you may only be insuring that you will be sent into battle if another war occurs in the next several years.

Even if there is no war in the immediate future, enlistment in the reserves is a major commitment. Most reservists are required to enlist for a period of at least six years. Anywhere from six months to two years of that time is spent on active duty. The remainder is spent attending "reserve meetings" one weekend each month, plus a full two weeks on active duty each year. Many reservists find such a schedule to be extremely stressful. They are civilians most of the time, but are required to play soldier or sailor during one full weekend each month in addition to spending their two week "vacation" on active duty each year.

A reservist who misses weekend reserve meetings can be punished by being placed on active duty for twenty-four months (less any active duty time already served) or for forty-five days (if he has already served two years or more on active duty). A reservist who does not report for the two-week activation each year can be court-martialled for being AWOL.

Another possibility some people consider is the National Guard. You should consider that Guard members, like reservists, are members of the military: Army National Guard members are in the Army, and Air National Guard members are in the Air Force. They are subject to a period of active duty (usually six months) and, like other reservists, are required to attend monthly meetings and annual activations under threat of permanent active duty assignment for missed meetings or courts-martial for missing activations.

While I don't recall any Guard members being sent to Vietnam, they could be called into any battle since they

36

are military reservists. In any event, many Guard members have found themselves activated to "control" anti-war and civil rights demonstrations at home. Could you aim a loaded gun at someone you work or go to school with, and fire if ordered? Many Guardsmen were ordered to do just that not so long ago.

What about the Coast Guard? Some people seem to feel that the Coast Guard is not a military organization, but look: they wear military uniforms, have military rank, hold military inspections, and are subject to military law, rules and regulations. In other words, the Coast Guard **is** a military organization. In the past several years the Coast Guard's biggest job has been making pot busts, but during the Vietnam war many of the Vietnamese rivers and deltas were regularly patrolled by Coast Guard cutters.

Enlistment promises and contracts

Military recruiters all have one thing in common: they are anxious to fill their quotas. As a result, many thousands of people have been enlisted illegally, and tens of thousands more have been enlisted legally but found that they weren't going to get what was promised to them by the recruiter. Military recruiters will often promise almost anything, but unless the promises appear in writing on the enlistment contract they are generally worthless. The usual principles of contract law often do not apply to military enlistment contracts, and even when they do apply the courts are prone to interpreting the contracts in favor of the military, not the individual soldier or sailor.

Promises that you will receive a particular kind of job training may be a joke. For instance, if you enlist to go to electronics school you may find yourself pulling wires instead of learning electronics. Recruiters have been known to enlist people for schools for which they are not qualified - being dropped from a military training school for academic

reasons **does not** void out your enlistment contract. You will be stuck for the rest of the enlistment period, and you can be assigned to whatever job the military wants to give you. You can bet it won't be a good one.

Even if you complete the training there is no guarantee that you will be allowed to work in your field - they may decide to assign you as a cook, supply sergeant, or even an infantryman on the front lines. Many of the "skills" taught in military schools have no civilian counter-part: how many classified ads have you seen lately looking for trained tank mechanics or missile guidance-system repairmen?

Guaranteed duty stations can also be a rip-off. Many men enlisted in the Army during Vietnam because they were promised they would be stationed in Germany or Hawaii, and that sounded better than Vietnam. Sure enough, they were sent to Germany or Hawaii . . . for ten months. Their **next** tour of duty was in lovely Southeast Asia where they could bask in the fragrant warmth of napalm fires.

The bottom line is that the military gives no guarantees that are permanent, and few that are even reliable. All members are expected to serve on the front lines at any time, any job or place of duty can be changed whenever "military convenience" dictates, reservists can be activated and active duty contracts can be involuntarily extended in times of "military mobilization," and enlistment contracts can be broken by the military almost at will

Tips for enlistees

If you are thinking of enlisting in the military, you would be well advised to protect yourself and keep the recruiters honest. Whenever you discuss things with a recruiter, have a witness with you. Get all promises in writing on the enlistment contract and initialled by the recruiter. Thoroughly read everything before you sign it. If there is anything you don't understand, take it to a civilian counselor or lawyer trained in military law. Don't believe the recruiter's explanation of what it means until you check it out with someone who isn't biased.

Find out what day-to-day life is like in the branch you are interested in by talking with other people (not recruiters) who are currently on active duty or have recently been in. If possible, talk with someone who has taken the school you are considering, or served in the location you have been promised, to see if your expectations are too high. A free trip to Europe at Army expense sounds wonderful but the realities of Army life in Europe can be grim.

Most importantly, explore your own needs and desires. Are you really ready to sign away two, three, four or more years of your life? Is the military the best thing for you to do right now? Will you still be willing to remain on active duty or in the reserves if a war starts up?

Far too many people enlist on the spur of the moment, and for poor reasons such as broken love affairs, fights with parents, or loss of a job. Those experiences last only a short while, but an enlistment contract lasts a long, long time. Think carefully before signing one. It is easy to enlist, but very difficult to change your mind once you are in.

40

REGISTRATION
AND RESISTANCE

The law says that all male US citizens and most resident aliens (non-US citizens) between the ages of eighteen and twenty-six can be required to register as the President may direct.[1] Currently the government has called for the registration of men born in 1960 and later years. Men born in 1960 and 1961 were required to register during the summer of 1980; those born in 1962, during January 1981. Men born in 1963 and later years must register within thirty days of their eighteenth birthday.[2]

The registration is done by use of forms available at Post Offices throughout the country, and at US Embassy offices in foreign countries.[3] If a man doesn't register when required to do so, he has broken the law.[4] The only exception is if he can show good reasons for not having registered, such as if he were hospitalized at the time.

While there are many people who think they will immediately be thrown into prison if they are caught for non-registration, the truth is that most people who have been caught in the past have never seen the inside of a courthouse, let alone a prison. This fear of prison is the image that Selective Service likes people to have. There is nothing that motivates people like fear, and that is one of the reasons people call Selective Service "the SS."

At this time there is no way to predict how the government is going to react to men who refuse to register, but there are certain assumptions we can make. No doubt some non-registrants will not be caught. Others will be caught and prosecuted. Some of them will be sent to prison, and some will receive probation sentences. Some "experts" predict leniency, while others fear severe punishment. Keep in mind that the government's purpose in using the draft law is to put people in uniform, not in jail. This does not mean that non-registrants won't be prosecuted, but possibly the government will not prosecute those who decide to register if caught and given the choice. Don't forget that late registration is also against the law, and could be charged up to five years after the individual finally registers.

Non-registration is breaking the law, and I certainly don't mean to encourage anyone to break the law. After all, that's illegal! But just for fun let's look at what it means to "break the law."

Laws are rules - guidelines for social conduct. Supposedly they reflect the ideal of the society, although sometimes they don't actually do so. It is doubtful whether many people really care whether they break a law or not. At one time or another almost everyone has run a stop sign, driven too fast, jay-walked, or somehow broken the law. What most people care about is whether or not they get caught breaking the law, and if caught what their penalty will be.

The maximum penalty for violating the draft law is five years in prison and/or a ten thousand dollar fine.[5] In reality monetary fines are rarely imposed, but contrary to "street rumors," prison sentences are **not** rare.

Some people have pointed to statistics from the Vietnam draft which show that only about ten percent of the men who violated the draft law were actually prosecuted,[6] but those figures are misleading. The vast majority of those cases involved men who refused to be inducted. Under the system then being used, it took months or years of processing by the system before an induction order could be issued. If a man could show that his induction order resulted from improper processing (which was often the case) he would not be prosecuted for refusing induction, but would be sent back to the local board for further processing. In many other cases a man who had refused induction would find that he had no legal defense to the charges. Rather than face conviction and a possible prison sentence, thousands of men agreed to accept induction if re-ordered, or to enlist in the military in order to avoid prosecution.

In other words, while nine out of ten cases were not prosecuted, very few draft law violators actually succeeded in avoiding the draft **and** avoiding prosecution.

The potential non-registrant should also consider that the Vietnam statistics are largely based on the charge of refusing induction. While no statistics are immediately available, most draft counselors and draft lawyers from that era agree that men who refused to register usually stood a much higher chance of being tried, convicted, and sentenced to prison than did those who registered on time but later chose to refuse induction. Again, this was due to the increased possibility of erroneous processing by Selective Service, which would give rise to a defense.

Leave the country?

People outside the country who do not register when required to do so are in violation of the draft law, the same as if they were inside the US. It is extremely unlikely that the FBI would bother to track down anyone outside the country who hasn't registered, and a person cannot usually be extradited to the United States for non-registration. However, anyone required to register who has not done so may run into troubles if he ever returns to US soil - which includes US embassies in other countries.

People who leave the United States after having registered will continue to be processed. Again, it is unlikely that a person would be extradited to the US for failure to comply with an induction order or other SS order, but if he ever returned to the US he would most likely be arrested and prosecuted. The same applies to anyone who refuses to register while in the US and later leaves the country.

However, a person who is not a United States citizen or resident alien at the time he would be required to register for the draft need not register. For instance, if a person left the United States at age seventeen and became (or already was) a citizen of some other country, he would not be required to register for the draft unless he later became a permanent resident alien, an illegal alien, or a United States citizen. It is possible that a person in this situation could return to the US at some later time, but such a tactic could result in his being denied US citizenship, and could even bar him from ever re-entering the US, even as a visitor. People considering this option should discuss it thoroughly with a lawyer who understands both draft law and immigration law.

Non-citizens who are currently living in the US, and dual nationals (citizens of both the US and some other country) are covered by several special provisions of the draft law. For more on that subject, see Appendix A.

Non-registration

If you decide not to register when required, there are some things that can better your odds of avoiding trial if caught, and also better your chances of avoiding prison if tried and convicted. The first question at hand, though, is what do you hope to accomplish by not registering? There are, of course, as many reasons for not registering as there are non-registrants. Since motives are sometime an important issue in court trials, no one should decide not to register without first deciding why he is refusing to register.

One point of view is that non-registration is a political statement: a man feels that the draft law is wrong, should not be allowed to exist, and therefore refuses to comply with it in any way. People who take this stand usually make public announcements of their non-registration and use every opportunity they can find to publicly denounce the draft. Of course, if you make your position public it is almost certain that the SS will eventually catch up with you, but that doesn't automatically mean you will end up in jail. In the past, most non-registrants were given at least one "warning," a notice that the SS had no record of their registration, and advising them to register immediately. If they decided at that time to register, they would usually just get put in with the other registrants. However, men who register late can still be prosecuted at some later time. Late registration may stall off **immediate** prosecution, but it does not erase the violation from your records.

On the other hand, if a man's conscience will not allow him to register, there is a possibility he will be taken to court, and perhaps sent to prison. I don't encourage people to go to prison. To the contrary, with so many options for avoiding the draft legally, I encourage people to comply with the law as far as their conscience will allow. However, one must respect those committed people who intelligently make the decision to take prison instead of the draft.

Another way to look at non-registration is to regard it as a more personal action. People who refuse to register for personal reasons may not be as concerned with political action as with their own situation or their own conscience. This is a perfectly respectable point of view.

Non-registration is not an easy way out

No one should fail to register because he thinks it is the "easy way out." There are many legal ways to avoid being drafted, but non-registration is **not** one of them. If you refuse to register, you are breaking the law, and that is not a game - it is a rugged way of life. Any refusal to cooperate with the SS, including non-registration, is known as resistance. You are taking a stand against the law, and you may go through hell for it.

Resistance is not a choice for people looking for an easy way out. It is a difficult road to travel, and a man taking it will probably have his life affected for years, perhaps forever. He stands a chance of ending up in prison for up to five years,[7] especially if he decides not to register even if caught. War resisters don't come out of jail as heroes; they come out as convicted felons.

People convicted of draft law violations lose many of their civil rights in most states. It is a felony, meaning that in many states they lose their right to vote, and may not be allowed to practice law or medicine. Some states, such as California, do not penalize draft law violators so harshly, since they look to see if a man's felony conviction involved "moral turpitude." But most states, and many major employers, are prejudiced against all felons.

Federal pens are no picnic, either. You will come into contact with some really hardened people . . . perverts, addicts, sadists, fascists, murderers, and so on. And those are just the guards - some of the prisoners are pretty bad, too.

Resistance is definitely not for the weak-at-heart, or for people who aren't sure what they want to do about the draft. Deciding to resist is a very real commitment. It is a decision that should be thought over very carefully. It is probably the biggest and most difficult decision a draft-age man has ever had to make. You should be sure you know what you are getting into before committing yourself to it, and should talk it over with someone you trust before making a final decision.

Going underground

Many people feel very dedicated to non-registration, but don't feel that they want to make their resistance public. Getting out of the draft by not registering can guarantee you a difficult future. It may mean the possibility of prosecution hanging over you for years to come. To avoid punishment, a person would have to avoid being arrested for many years. If you were to decide not to register, and also not to make your act a public statement, and assuming you wanted to avoid getting caught for as long as possible, then you may want to know how others in your situation have handled the problem. Once again, I want to make it clear that I do not advise anyone to break the law.

Some people, while not being overtly public, are still so proud of their non-registration that they let on (brag) to people they know that they haven't registered. This is fine if a man wants to take a public stand, but it is a damned poor way to keep a secret. Sooner or later the wrong person is going to hear about it and "patriotically" turn him in. Or someone will have a grievance with him and "get even" by turning him in. Ironically, the majority of non-registrants who do get caught are turned in by family members or ex-lovers.

Other non-registrants seem to become paranoid. They turn pale if anyone mentions the draft. They run and hide if they see a policeman. They change jobs often and are constantly on the move, even though no one is actually after them. They are always looking over their shoulders, and don't trust people. They become loners. Their behavior is often so suspicious that people become suspicious of them, fulfilling their own fears, sometimes causing them to eventually get caught.

One of the more common ways for non-registrants to be caught is by being arrested for some other charge. Even being stopped for running a stop sign or having a faulty automobile tail light could result in a police check on your name. If the computer bank shows that you may be a non-registrant, you will suddenly have problems far more serious than running a stop sign.

Another possible catch for non-registrants comes from schools. Some high schools and colleges perform a "public service" by sending the SS and military recruiters a list of students. If you received a rash of recruiting literature at about the time you graduated from high school, there is a good chance that the system knows you exist. This means it will be easy for them to track you down. Consequently, you may find yourself moving around a lot, and developing all the paranoid tendencies described above. It's no fun!

People who do register for the draft will be assigned a Selective Service number by the SS. That number will be used to identify all correspondence with the registrant, and for that reason most registrants will know their Selective Service number, or at least will know how to find it. The man who decides not to register will not have an SS number, and that could lead to some embarrassing results, such as arrest.

If caught

Let's imagine that, despite all precautions, you are caught for non-registration. As mentioned earlier, most people caught in the past for non-registration have been given a choice: register or face trial. If a person decides to register at that point he won't automatically be drafted - he will be put in with the rest of the registrants born in his year of birth and treated exactly the same as everyone else. Of course, someone will probably want to know why he didn't register on time. It may be that, as a matter of conscience, he didn't feel that he could be a part of the war machine, but has now decided that his registering won't necessarily

48

mean being a part of it. If so, he may be qualified for a conscientious objector classification, and want to explain that in writing.

In any event, the system wants people to register. The SS is likely to accept just about any reason given for late registration. Some lawyers, including myself, contend that a person doesn't have to provide a statement explaining his late registration. By simply supplying the system with what it needs to register him, he is fulfilling his legal obligation. People who decide to give a reason should realize that even though they are being allowed to register late, they can still be prosecuted for late registration up to five years later.[8] Any statement they make concerning their late registration could later be used as evidence against them.

A great number of non-registrants turn themselves in after a year or two. The case of one such person is worth telling. He was born on December 10, 1952, and was required to register during December, 1970. The holiday season came and passed, and by mid-January, 1971, he came to the realization that he had become a non-registrant. On August 5, 1971, when his lottery number was drawn, he paid little attention to it. But a few weeks later a friend (not knowing that this fellow had not registered) congratulated him on getting lottery number 362. After some quick thinking, our hero went down to the old SS building and explained that he had been waiting over nine months and still hadn't received his registration papers and wondered what he should do. Seeing that he was just a "dumb innocent kid" of eighteen, the motherly clerk explained to him that he was supposed to have come in to register, and that the system did not send out papers to potential registrants. He expressed his surprise, filled out a sheet of paper explaining why he was late, and got himself registered. Since a lottery cut-off number well below his had already been announced, he was relatively sure of not being drafted.

Registration procedure

Registration procedures may seem a bit anti-climactic after all this discussion of resistance, but your best chance for a happy future means that you first have to get properly and legally registered. Then you start working to get things to come out the way you want them to.

Registration for the draft is currently being handled by Post Offices. The actual process consists of providing the SS with enough information to allow them to locate you if and when they decide to draft you. A form is provided for you to fill out. It asks for your name, sex, date of birth, social security number, current phone number, and two addresses - a current mailing address and permanent residence. One of those addresses, probably the current mailing address, will be used to assign you to a local board. This is the board that will decide on your requests for deferment, exemption, change of classification, and so on.

As a rule of thumb, a rural draft board is less likely to grant deferments and exemptions than an urban board. Naturally, no draft board is great, but some are worse than others. People with a choice of addresses may want to consider which address will net them a "better" local board, and provide only that address on their registration form.

Some registrants have been known to provide the address of a friend or relative as their official address in order to get a more reasonable local board. That seems to be perfectly legal, as long as the people at the address given will **regularly** and **promptly** get your mail to you.

Some registrants have provided false addresses when registering. Not only is that illegal, it could also work against you. There are many times when you can preserve your rights **only** if you respond to mail sent out by the SS within a very short time, such as ten or fifteen days from mailing. Providing a false address will mean missing deadlines and losing advantages that might have been gained.

It is important for you to understand that you are legally responsible for receiving your mail from the SS, and that the Post Office is forbidden by law from forwarding mail from them to you, even if you have filled out a change of address notice. You **must** keep the SS notified of an address where you can be sure of receiving any mail they may send.

There is no reason why the registration form must be filled out right there in the Post Office. In fact, it would seem to make a great deal of sense to take the form to a draft counselor and discuss how to answer the questions posed. That is especially true if a person has a choice of addresses, or wishes to pursue ultimate deferment or exemption from the draft.

Another point to bear in mind is that you don't have to appear for registration at the Post Office which covers the area where your local board will be. For instance, let's say that your mailing address is San Francisco, but you are currently going to school in Chicago. You could show up at any Post Office in Chicago, fill out the form, and be registered. As long as you give only the San Francisco address on your registration form, you will be assigned to a San Francisco local board.

The registration form itself does not contain any opportunity to claim deferment or exemption from the draft. However, that should not slow down the enterprising draft registrant. Let's say a fellow is interested in being classified as a conscientious objector, and wishes to take every available opportunity to inform the SS of his feelings. When he is required to register, he takes with him a broad-tipped felt pen. On the registration form he finds some available space and writes in the words "I am a conscientious objector". That way, if he is a conscientious objector, or if he is unsure whether or not he is a conscientious objector, or if he thinks he might become a conscientious objector if the system tries to draft him, or for any other reason he feels so inclined, he has begun to set up some documentation of his claim.

Before turning a completed registration form over to a Postal clerk, you would be well advised to make at least two photocopies of the form as filled out, including any statements on the form about being qualified for a deferment or exemption. If possible, you should have a witness accompany you to the Post Office when the form is turned in. There are two reasons for making copies and having a witness:

First: Postal employees have been instructed not to give any receipts for completed registration forms. If the Post Office manages to lose it, or if the SS somehow fails to get the information properly programmed into its computer, you will have no proof that you registered. But, if you have a photocopy of the registration form, and a witness who saw you turn in the original, you will have proof. To play really safe, you should have your witness indicate on one photocopy that the witness saw you hand in the original form at a stated Post Office, and the witness should date and sign the photocopy. That copy can then be placed in an envelope and mailed to you. The envelope should not be opened or tampered with when it is delivered. If any question ever arises as to whether you registered when required to do so, the postmarked, **sealed** envelope containing the photocopy and the witness's statement can be presented to a judge. That should provide more than enough proof.

Second: Even if no trouble comes up about your having registered on time, the witnessed photocopy can serve another purpose. Once the SS computerizes the information on your registration form, the original form will most likely be destroyed. If you claimed on the registration form that you are a conscientious objector, that information will **not** be fed into the SS computer. Once the form is destroyed, you will have no proof that you registered as a conscientious objector unless you kept a copy of the form. Further, the fact that the copy of the form is contained in a post-marked, sealed envelope dated the same day you registered provides proof that your original registration form really did indicate your conscientious objection. This way there can be no suspicion that you might have later filled out a registration form saying you are a conscientious objector.

The Post Office will send the registration form to the SS, where the information will be fed into a computer. The only communication from the SS after registration will be a form letter sent out within ninety days after you register. The letter will acknowledge that you have registered, ask whether the information shown in the computer is correct, inform you of your legal duty to keep the SS informed of an address where mail will reach you, and assign you a Selective Service number. The SS number will be used to identify you, and should be kept, since it will be needed on all further communications with the SS, including any subsequent changes of address. If you find that the information fed into the computer is incorrrect, you should notify the SS as soon as possible. And if you feel that the error in SS records is that it fails to reflect that you claimed to be a conscientious objector when you registered, you may wish to inform the SS of that fact. It probably won't force them to keep records on people who claim to be conscientious objectors, but by once again making a photocopy of the communication and mailing a copy to yourself, you will start building your conscientious objector file.

In the event that more than ninety days pass after you register and you do not receive the form letter from the

SS, you should immediately write a letter to them asking what has happened to your registration information. Once again, a photocopy of the letter should be kept, although it is not necessary that you mail yourself a copy of it.

For more hints on building a Selective Service file, please see the section on Communicating With The SS in Chapter 11.

Under the computerized SS process no "draft files" will be set up, and there will be no official opportunity to submit evidence to support a claim for any deferment or exemption. Only basic information will be kept, and it will all be computerized.

Resistance after registration

Registering does not mean that you absolutely will be drafted. It merely means that you **may** be drafted. You could get a high lottery number and not be called; you might qualify for one of several deferments or exemptions which will keep you from being drafted; or you may be able to find other ways to avoid ever being called.

For many people who make the decision to register, their set of circumstances after registration brings with it the realization that they no longer care to cooperate with the system. Many of them decide to do what they can, legally or otherwise, to "jam" the system. The following discussion is not intended to encourage people to do illegal acts, but merely to report things which others have done in the past.

A man has a legal duty to keep the SS informed of an address where mail will reach him.[9] That does not mean that you must report a change of address every time you move, as long as the address they have is one where mail will reach you. Even if you are working or going to school hundreds of miles from the address the SS has, you are legal so long as someone at that address will receive mail for you and send it along, or let you know when it arrives. However, if the address given to the SS is no good, or becomes no good, a failure to give them a valid address is a violation of the law punishable by up to five years in prison and/or a $10,000 fine. Mail from the SS may not legally be forwarded by the Post Office, even if you have given the Post Office a change of address form. You **must** notify the SS directly. As discussed above, a change of address could mean a change in your draft board.

Some people have used address changes to jam the system. One man I know gave his parents' address when he registered, and shortly after that time he moved into an apartment a few miles away. No matter which of those addresses the SS used he would be assigned to the same local board, since there was only one local board serving his entire county. And no matter which of those addresses the SS used, mail would reach him.

He realized that every time he reported a change of address, someone would have to change some SS records (and under the computerized system, would also have to feed new data to the computer). He just couldn't decide which address to use, and ended up changing his address every few months. Soon a number of his friends became as indecisive as he was, and it became a full time job for the SS to keep track of all their different address changes. If you want to keep the system running smoothly you are going to have to try not to change addresses as often as those fellows did.

In addition to indecisive people, the world contains many people who have poor memories. Some can't remember names, others forget birthdays and anniversaries, while others can't seem to recall even the most important things . . . such as whether or not they remembered to register for the draft. These poor souls will drift through life in a fog. They will wake up in the morning and wonder aloud, "Gosh, did I register for the draft?"

There may be help for these unfortunates. It may well be that a simple letter to the SS, asking whether or not they did register, will receive a response reassuring them that they did. Of course, it will take someone in the SS a little time to check the computer to see whether or not a man has registered - especially if he can't even recall his SS number. And it will take a little more time to write him a letter assuring him that all is well. But nothing is too good for our boys. And, golly, if the poor devil forgets again six months later, and again writes in to make absolutely sure that he really honestly did register for the draft, I guess the SS will just have to let him know again. And again. And again.

Whether or not to register for the draft, and once registered whether or not to resist, are not easy decisions. They should be given a great deal of thought. It may be that discussing these things with relatives, friends, ministers or draft counselors will make the decisions easier, but the final decision is yours, and yours alone. It is your life, and no one else can decide for you.

PART TWO: THE MIDDLE GAME

CLASSIFICATION

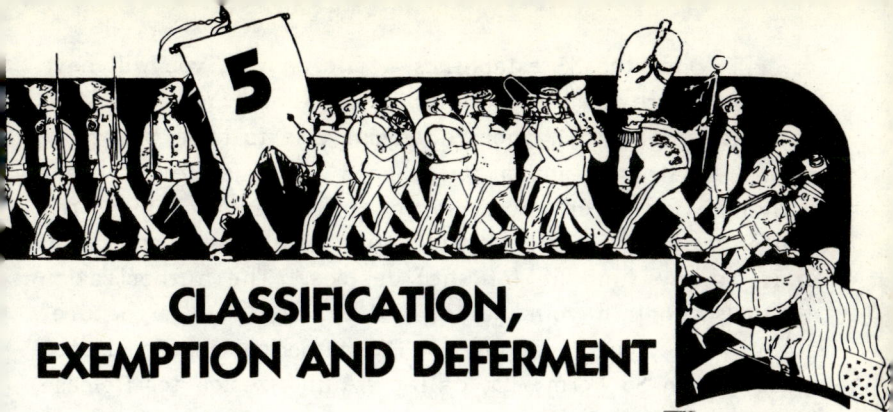

CLASSIFICATION, EXEMPTION AND DEFERMENT

At present there are no local boards and no one is being classified. Under the President's proposed plan, no one will be classified until drafting begins, but that can happen very suddenly, at any time. When drafting does begin, **all** draft registrants will be **presumed** to be classified 1-A for purposes of sending out induction orders.

As soon as a draft is ordered, local boards will quickly be set up, induction orders will begin going out, and the classification process will begin immediately.[1] Each draft board will be provided the names, addresses, dates of birth and other information about draft-age men in their locality, and individual files will be set up for each registrant.[2] A man's draft file will contain any information he submits, such as applications for deferment or exemption, as well as any other information the SS has on him, such as results of physical examinations at AFEES, information about him submitted by other people, and so on.[3] There was a time when the SS was required to keep **anything** a registrant sent them, but people started sending in old tires, bricks, packages of garbage, and so on. The regulations were quickly changed, and when local boards resume operations they will be authorized to throw away anything that is considered irrelevant or duplicative. In other words, they will not be required to keep that 4' x 8' piece of plywood you send them, unless, of course, it has your conscientious objector application written on it, in which case they will probably be required to keep it. And they will probably find a reason to deny your claim for conscientious objector status as well.

Once the SS establishes a file on you, you will have the right to review its contents at any time.[4] You will also have the right to authorize anyone else to have that same right.[5] A letter of authorization need merely state: "I hereby authorize (whoever you wish to authorize) to review the contents of my Selective Service file, and to copy any or all of it at any time he (or she) desires." The authorization must also contain your name, a date, and your signature, along with your SS number.[6] The authorization can also be made out on SS Form 725, called "Authorization for Release of Information".

Certain groups of people have been known to authorize one another to have access to each other's draft files, and then go to the local board office in a group and take turns reading files. Of course, that practice tends to jam up the system and make it difficult for the clerks to attend to the real business of drafting people.

But I am digressing. We are at the point where drafting has resumed, lottery numbers have been assigned, and local board offices have been set up.

After you have been assigned a lottery number, the next step in being processed by the SS is known as classification. You will be classified by your local board. If your lottery number is higher than the expected ceiling for the year (see Chapter 2) or if a Second Priority Group is established immediately, you will likely be classified 1-H and will not have to deal with the draft any further. On the other hand, if your lottery number is below the ceiling number, or if no ceiling number is set for the year, you will be processed soon after the lottery is drawn. Those with the lowest lottery numbers will likely receive an induction order prior to any classification processing taking place.

Bear in mind that under the proposed mobilization standards all draft registrants will be presumed to be classified 1-A **unless** they submit a claim for deferment or exemption.[7]

Deferments & exemptions

Each draft registrant will be placed into one of twenty-two classifications, and his classification will determine whether or not he is subject to being drafted.

Whenever a local board classifies anyone, there is a procedure set out in the SS regulations that they must follow. If you have claimed to be eligible for any deferment or exemption, especially if you have claimed conscientious objector status or an extreme hardship deferment, the local board **must** send you the appropriate form and allow you to fill it out and return it.[8] If you have already been sent an order to report for induction, it must be cancelled or postponed,[9] although you may still be required to report for a physical exam on the appointed day. Next, your entire file must be presented to the local board for consideration. Based on the information in the file, the board must decide which classification to give you.[10] If the board turns down a requested deferment or exemption it must state its reasons, and those reasons must appear in writing and be supported by information in your file.[11]

The law states that the local board **must** consider a man for and place him in the **lowest** classification that he is eligible for.[12]

Listed below are the twenty-two classifications which Selective Service will be using, along with a short explanation of what each classification means and reference to the parts of this book where it is discussed more fully. The list is in order of priority as established by the SS; that is, 1A is highest priority, first to go, and 1C is lowest and last.

I-A Fully eligible for induction into military service. Under the President's proposal, **all** draft registrants will be **presumed** 1-A. Those with low lottery numbers will be ordered for induction first, and then allowed a short time in which to claim some other classification.

1–AM Medical specialist fully eligible for induction into military service. (Chapter 10.)

1–A–O Conscientious objector willing to go into military service as a non-combatant, but not as a combatant member. (Chapter 6.)

1–A–OM Medical specialist 1-A-O conscientious objector. (Chapters 6 & 10.)

1–O Conscientious objector opposed to any kind of military seervice, but willing to do civilian work contributing to the national health, safety or interest. (Chapter 6.)

1–OM Medical specialist 1-O conscientious objector. (Chapters 6 & 10.)

2–AM Medical doctor, dentist, optometrist, osteopath, podiatrist, veterinarian or registered nurse whose occupation represents a critical community service. (Chapter 10.) Deferment.

2–D Student of theology satisfactorily pursuing studies preparing him for the ministry. (Chapter 9.) Deferment.

3–A Registrant with one or more dependents whose dependents would suffer hardship economically, physically or emotionally if he were drafted. (Chapter 7.) Deferment.

4–B Judges and certain federal and state elected officials. Exemption.

4-C Non-US citizens and dual nationals who are exempt from the draft, currently outside the US, or have been in the US less than one year. (Appendix A.) Exemption.

4-D Full time or regularly practicing minister of religion. (Chapter 9.) Exemption.

4-G Person whose father, brother or sister died as a result of injury or disease incurred while in the military. (Chapter 8.) Exemption.

1-H Administrative holding classification for people whose lottery number is above the expected ceiling, or people who for some other reason are not being processed at the time. (Chapter 2.)

4-F Not qualified for any service, either military or as a conscientious objector, because of medical, mental or administrative reasons. (Chapter 14.) Exemption.

2-M Medical student preparing to be a medical doctor, dentist, optometrist, osteopath, podiatrist, veterinarian or registered nurse. (Chapter 10.) Deferment.

4-FM Medical specialist not qualified for service because of medical, mental or administrative reasons. (Chapter 10 & 14.) Exemption.

4-W Conscientious objector who has completed civilian alternate service work. (Chapter 6.)

4-A People who have completed military service, including non-US citizens and dual citizens of some countries who have completed military service in their own country. (Appendix A.) Exemption.

I-D Member of the military Reserves, National Guard, or advanced ROTC training. Deferment.

I-W Conscientious objector currently performing civilian alternate service. (Chapter 6.)

I-C Active members of the military, commissioned officers of the Public Health Service or the National Oceanic and Atmospheric Administration.

The SS likes to give the public the impression that 1-A is the classification they give men only if they can't find any other classification they qualify for. But the fact of the matter is that the job of a local board is to draft people. Members of the board would quickly be asked to resign (or perhaps even be prosecuted) if they were primarily interested in granting a deferment or exemption to everyone who came along. If you want a classification other than 1-A, you can probably get it, but you may have to work for it, and for some of you it may be very hard work.

In the following chapters, there is a detailed discussion of the various exemptions and deferments, with tips on how to get the one you want. Chapter 11 tells you what to do if you don't get your way.

CONSCIENTIOUS OBJECTION

One of the most talked-about aspects of the draft is Conscientious Objection, commonly called CO status. It seems that just about everyone knows that there is such a thing, but very few people understand what it is really all about.

Some people seem to think that filing for CO status is an easy and automatic was to "get out" of the draft. If you have read this far, you know that the SS is not about to give people an easy way out. Conscientious objectors are subject to being drafted. The difference is that a man drafted as a CO doesn't have to put in two years as a combat member of the military.

To qualify for classification as a conscientious objector a person must show that his deeply and sincerely held religious, moral or ethical beliefs cause him to feel opposed to taking part in all war in any form.[1] Naturally it isn't quite as easy as just writing that sentence on a piece of paper and sending it to a draft board, but that definition sums it up in a nutshell.

A conscientious objector is subject to being called in the same way as other draft registrants: his lottery number must be reached while he is a member of the First Priority Group (see Chapter 2) and he must be found physically acceptable.[2] The physical fitness standards for conscientious objectors are exactly the same as for 1-A draftees, and since the 4-F medical exemption is a lower classification than either of the conscientious objector classifications (see Chapter 5), anyone who is found to be physically unacceptable doesn't have to worry about qualifying as a CO because he can't be drafted anyway.[3] But a conscientious objector who qualifies for no other deferment or exemption will be subject to the draft, if and when his lottery number is reached..

There are two conscientious objector classifications used by the SS: 1-A-O and 1-O, and when filing for CO status a man is supposed to choose one or the other. Some people do not feel that they can accept either classification, since neither one really defines their feelings, or since they object to the "right" of the SS to classify people at all. While these are admirable and valid opinions, CO claims based on such reasons are not likely to be approved. Any conscientious objector who feels that he can not accept either CO classification offered by the SS should work closely with a lawyer.

1-A-O and 1-O conscientious objection

A 1-A-O classification is available for those conscientious objectors who object to taking part in combat, but are willing to enter the military in some non-combatant job.[4] Of the two CO classifications, the 1-A-O is the easier to get, since a 1-A-O draftee will go into the military and thereby fill the draft quota. However, no one should request 1-A-O status simply because it is easier to obtain -- you should file only for the status you really want. While both classifications require similar kinds of proof, a 1-A-O who later requests 1-O status stands a poor chance of success, and in fact could even lose his 1-A-O status in the process.

If granted 1-A-O status and then drafted, a man will go into the military as a non-combatant. He will still have to go through complete military training and orientation, but will not be given arms training and will not be forced to bear arms. In addition, he will be trained to do a non-combat military job. The overwhelming majority of 1-A-O draftees during Vietnam were trained to be medics.

There is absolutely nothing in draft or military law to keep a 1-A-O from being sent into a combat zone or working on the front lines. If he has been trained as a medic, the odds are extremely high that that is precisely where he will end up. After all, that is where medics are needed.

The basic differences between being drafted as a 1-A draftee or as a 1-A-O is that the 1-A-O will not have to carry or use firearms. Both are in uniform,, both are sworn to support the military and its missions, and both are subject to all military rules and regulations. The 1-A-O will not be called upon to kill, but there is nothing to prevent him from being injured or killed.

Some conscientious objectors feel that they can enter the military as medics because it is a humanitarian job to assist the wounded. For other objectors, a close look at the realities of being a part of the war effort causes them to take a different view. In medic school, for example, one is taught that the job of a medic is to patch up soldiers, not necessarily to heal their wounds, but to send them out to fight again. The military medic policy is often to treat the **least injured** first, since they have the best chance of a speedy return to battle.

Many conscientious objectors feel that there is no real difference between ordering bombs and dropping them, or between killing someone and assisting someone else to kill them. For conscientious objectors who feel that they can not serve in the military in any way, there is the 1-O classification.[5]

If drafted as a 1-O, a man will be called for the same period of time as anyone else who is drafted - two years. The big difference is that instead of being called for military duty, a 1-O is required to perform two years of civilian work that is approved by the SS. This is known as civilian alternate service work.[6] Many of the approvable jobs are very menial and uncreative, such as working as a hospital orderly, driving a truck for Goodwill Industries, and so on. But there are some decent jobs which a 1-O can have approved, and upon being ordered into civilian alternate service work a 1-O has an opportunity to locate his own job and submit it to the SS for approval.

Of course, being drafted as a 1-O is still being drafted. But to many people being drafted to work in the civilian community for two years seems a whole lot better than being drafted to carry a gun and fight.

Who qualifies?

A conscientious objector is someone whose conscience would give him no peace if he took part in warfare. In the past only "religious objectors" were recognized. If a man wasn't a member of a recognized "peace church", such as the Quakers or Mennonites, he was pretty much out of luck. But two important Supreme Court decisions[7] have expanded the meaning of the word "religious" to include any strongly held moral or ethical belief. In other words, a man no longer has to belong to a church or believe in a God to be classified as a conscientious objector, as long as he feels very strongly that participation in war is wrong. The Supreme Court definition of a conscientious objector is someone whose deeply and sincerely held religious, moral or ethical beliefs cause him to be opposed to taking part in all war in any form.[8]

People who feel that a particular war or particular kind of war (such as oil wars, nuclear wars, and so on) is wrong, but feel that they would fight in some other wars, do not qualify as conscientious objectors under current law.[9] Also, anyone whose reasons for objecting to war are political (the US has no right to be an imperialist nation), sociological (it is wrong for this society to waste its healthy men) or pragmatic (I don't want to get injured or killed) are not qualified as concientious objectors.[10] Mind you, I feel that those are all very valid views which would cause a person to be opposed to war, but I am not your local draft board. The point is that the SS won't accept those reasons as a basis for a CO claim, and if a person wants his claim granted he is going to have to play by their rules.

If a person feels morally compelled to push for "selective objection" to a particular war, or political conscience as a basis for a CO claim, more power to him. But be aware that others have tried it before, and many ended up in jail for their beliefs.

A person need not be a pacifist to qualify as a conscientious objector. Conscientious objectors may believe in self-defense or defense of their loved ones, but still be opposed to taking part in war.[11] It is not necessary to convince the SS that your beliefs are **right**, but only that you sincerely hold those beliefs and live by them. One man who was born and raised on a Pacific island based his CO claim on the belief that God lived in a volcano on his homeland. The local board may not have been converted to his religious beliefs, but they did find him to sincerely hold those beliefs and granted his 1-O request.

The SS has a form (Selective Service Form 150) designed for use by conscientious objectors. It contains six questions about the applicant's beliefs and how those beliefs relate to his feelings about war. The questions are not easy to answer, and may take weeks or even months of consideration. There are no "right" answers, since each person's beliefs are going to be slightly different. But there are some "wrong" answers, in the sense that some kinds of responses will virtually assure a denial of the claim.

Putting together a legally sufficient response to Form 150 can be a long and difficult task. Anyone who intends to file as a conscientious objector should obtain a copy of Form 150 from a local SS office (as soon as they are set up) or study the one shown in this chapter, and work on his application long before it is demanded by the SS. Throwing together a claim under the pressure of a ten or fifteen day deadline could result in denial of an otherwise valid claim. Draft counselors have copies of Form 150 available, along with literature about conscientious objection. They can also help people to think through their feelings about war, and to put together an application for conscientious objector status that will avoid the more common pitfalls and stand a better chance of approval by the local board.

The six questions

The first question on Form 150 asks: "Describe the beliefs which are the basis for your claim for classification as a conscientious objector." It calls for a person's basic religious, moral or ethical beliefs. Do you believe in God? If so, what are the teachings of the God? If you do not believe in a God, what code of ethics or set of morals do you use to guide your life? A response to this question should not be confined to a discussion of warfare, but should also include an outline of **all** your beliefs. For instance, a member of a traditional Christian religion might include a discussion of his belief in the Ten Commandments, the Golden Rule, and so on.

The second question asks: "Will your beliefs permit you to serve in a position in the armed forces where the use of weapons is not required? If not, why?" For the 1-A-O objector, a simple "yes" answer will suffice. For the 1-O objector, the question gets more involved. This is where it must be shown that **any** participation in the military, whether directly combatant or non-combatant, would violate the conscience of the applicant.

Question three asks: "Explain how you acquired the beliefs which are the basis of your claim." This is largely an historical question wanting to know what life experiences, including any formal religious training, have led you to believe as you do. Bear in mind that it asks for the development not only of anti-war beliefs, but all beliefs stated in response to question number one.

Question four asks: "Explain what most clearly shows that your beliefs are deeply held." The most common answer is that filing for CO status shows that the man's beliefs are deeply held. Not only is the logic of that answer questionable, but the frequency with which it is used causes draft boards (and even me) to be bored with it. You should describe events in your life that show that you live consistently with the beliefs you stated under question one. For instance, if you stated a belief in the Ten Commandments, you could describe incidents showing that you do not take the Lord's name in vain, that you honor your parents, that you do not covet your neighbor's goods . . . and, of course, that you do not kill.

Questions five and six actually pose three questions which all boil down to asking the applicant to expand on what he said in response to question four. The three questions are: "(5) Do your beliefs affect the way you live? Describe how your beliefs affect the type of work you will do to earn a living or the types of activities you participate in during nonworking hours. (6) Describe any specific actions or incidents in your life that show you believe as you do."

Although these questions seem to ask for silly answers, such as listing anti-war activities, patting one's own back, or speculating on whether one would work for a war industry, it is important to try to answer them fully. The response to these questions will be just about the only thing the local board will use in determining whether your beliefs are deeply and sincerely held. During Vietnam, "lack of sincerity" was one of the most common reasons given by local boards for denying CO claims.

The six questions can be answered separately, or an applicant can submit a single essay which covers all six questions. The actual process of filing for CO status, along with copies of Form 150, are contained in the "Handbook For Conscientious Objectors," published by the Central Committee for Conscientious Objectors, whose addresses are listed in the back of this book.

When to file

The law requires a person to file as a CO within ten days of the time that he realizes he is a conscientious objector.[12] However, since no process is provided by the SS for filing until after one receives an induction order, and since no local boards currently exist, it is currently impossible for conscientious objectors to file their claims with the SS. The courts have ruled that "late filing" alone does not indicate insincerity,[13] and since no applications are currently being accepted, there is no such thing as "late filing". Nonetheless, a person who files at the earliest opportunity is going to stand a better chance of having his claim granted than a man who waits until the last minute. For that reason, the following process is suggested.

If you know at the time you register for the draft that you are a conscientious objector, or even if you just think you **might** be a conscientious objector, then you should write on your registration form the words "I am a conscientious objector". A photocopy of the form should be made, mailed back to yourself, and kept unopened in the sealed envelope until needed. If at some later date you are processed for induction and submit a claim for conscientious objector status, the sealed and postmarked envelope will be proof that you "registered" as a conscientious objector months or years before.

In mid-1971 the Supreme Court ruled that the SS does not have to process a CO claim which is presented after an induction order is issued.[14] But changes in the SS regulations, and the President's proposal to delay all claims until after induction orders are issued, will undoubtedly change that law. (See Chapter 1 for information about the President's proposed "mobilization" plans.) Current SS regulations[15] do allow a person under a "postponed" or "cancelled" induction order to file a CO claim, as long as no new date has been set for him to report for induction. Presumably if you receive an induction order and indicate your conscientious objection within the ten days allowed, your induction will be postponed or cancelled to allow you to file your claim. People who indicate when registering that they are conscientious objectors may also have an automatic right to postponement or cancellation of any induction order sent to them, since a person who has filed as a conscientious objector can not be ordered for induction until his claim has been settled. However, since the "filing" at registration was not official, no one should neglect to re-affirm their conscientious objection if issued an induction order or given any other official means of doing so by the SS.

Alternate service work

Despite the fact that most alternate service work tends to be menial and low-paying or non-paying, there are redeeming factors. For one thing, if you obtain a 1-O classification and get called to do alternate service work, you will be given a sixty day period in which to locate a job that you want to do, and submit it to the SS for approval.[16] Believe it or not, there are some approved or approvable

73

jobs that aren't too bad, and a few that are very good. Some civil service positions are approved, free clinics sometimes qualify, some forms of social work, especially in poor or minority communities, may qualify, and there are even some approved jobs working in foreign countries with religious or social groups.

In addition to "traditionally approved" jobs, the SS is always open to new jobs, so even if the job you would like to do has never before been approved, it may be that you and your prospective employer can present the job to the SS in a way that will get the system to approve it.

Almost all approved alternate service jobs pay very little, since they are required to be in the national health, safety or interest, which usually translates into working for a non-profit organization. But there are at least some jobs where a person can feel creative and positive. In the past, some counseling agencies have had CO job counseling available, including lists of approved or potentially approvable jobs in the area.

If you are called for alternate service work and do not find an acceptable job within the sixty day period the SS will assign you a job.[17] You can bet that if you wait for a "work order" to be issued you are going to be assigned to the lousiest job they can come up with. If you refuse to comply with a work order, you can be prosecuted just the same as if you had refused to comply with an induction order.[18] The difference is that people convicted of refusing to comply with a work order stand a stronger chance of being sent to prison than those who refuse induction. Apparently the courts feel that a conscientious objector has already "been given a break".

In the past it was worth bearing in mind that a work order to a specific job didn't necessarily mean that there was work available with that employer. Many times people under work orders travelled hundreds of miles to comply, only to find that the employer had no position available. One way to avoid being ripped off by the SS like that is to explain to the local board that you will comply with the order, but that you can't afford the travel expenses. According to SS regulations, the SS must provide transportation expenses to any 1-O ordered for civilian work.[19] Several objectors have used that provision to insist that their local board arrange for their transportation when they have been ordered to a place distant from their place of residence. They sometimes further demanded that the SS guarantee them, in writing, that return passage will be paid for by the SS if work is not available at that location for at least six weeks. Some boards found it easier to cancel the work order than to comply with the regulations.

Of those boards that did guarantee transportation cost requests, some had occasion to get upset when some CO would show up thoroughly refreshed by his vacation, demanding return busfare because there was no job available. There have even been reports that some conscientious objectors did not even bother to take the trip. They cashed in their bus ticket (paid for by the SS) and placed a long-distance call to the employer. When told that the employer was not hiring, they asked that he or she send them a letter to that effect. When they got the letter, they took it to their local board and demanded return busfare. Such a practice is, of course, highly illegal and should not be done. It is not nice to rip off the SS for a couple hundred dollars, and besides, you might get caught and go to jail for doing it.

Other objectors, especially those who were gainfully employed when ordered to report for alternate service work, seemed to find great difficulty in getting hired by an alternate service employer. They reported for job after job, but kept getting turned down. That is not difficult to understand, since many Vietnam-era objectors were dirty hippies who never bathed or shaved, and always wore old tattered clothing. I mean, would you want your sister to work with one? Heavens, no! Fortunately for some objectors, neither did some employers.

In California and Washington the scarcity of jobs for conscientious objectors and the inability of some objectors to be hired was countered by the establishment of an "Ecology Corps". Several old prison camps were re-opened and staffed, sometimes by prison guards. While the name "Ecology Corps" seemed to imply a concern for the environment, these camps were actually just a cheap way to procure fire-fighters. Reports from objectors in the California Ecology Corps indicated that they were more like prison camps or concentration camps than the "volunteer" organizations they were supposed to be. There were some reports of brutality, and many reports of forced hair-cutting. It is unclear how alternate service work will be administered in the future, but I suspect that the "Ecology Corps" experiment may have paved the way for similar CO work camps in the future.

Some points for 1-O's to consider

The processing of a claim for CO status is basically the same as the processing of any claim requesting deferment or exemption. (More about that process can be found in Chapters 11, 12 and 13.) When filing for 1-O status, there are some additional tactics that may be helpful to know.

You should be sure to take advantage of all of your appeal rights, for several reasons:
1) Any time that you fail to make full use of your appeal rights, you are limiting the chances of having your claim granted.
2) By not showing up for a personal appearance with the local board, or by not requesting a State appeal, you may bring question on your sincerity as a CO.

3) The courts are sometimes called upon to review CO claims. That usually happens after an objector's claim is denied and he has been ordered for induction, but he refuses to be inducted. As a defense, it is possible to argue that the induction order should not have been issued, since the man should have been classified 1-O, and of course a 1-O is not inducted. However, the courts have a rule that before they will look into whether a 1-O should have been granted, the defendant must first show that he made every possible attempt to have the SS grant his claim, **including full use** of his appeals rights within the SS.[20] The man who fails to use those rights may not be allowed to argue his objection to the judge, and may end up being convicted even though the local board denied his CO claim illegally.

As discussed in Chapter 13, there is no further appeal from an appeal board **if** their decision is unanimous. But even if you are turned down unanimously by the appeal board, it still may be possible to avoid an induction order. The State and National SS Directors have the power to request a National Appeal on your behalf regardless of the vote of the appeal board.[21] Sending them copies of your CO file and requesting their intervention may be helpful. You may do that directly, or with assistance from a sympathetic member of Congress.

If you submit substantial new evidence in support of your claim, the local board **must** consider it, and they may be forced to re-open your classification and give you an entire new set of appeal rights.[22]

Some objectors find that there is no relief in sight, and when ordered for induction they decide to refuse to enter the military rather than to violate their conscience. Statistics, for what they are worth, show that objectors who refuse induction after trying **every** other way to get a valid CO claim granted stand about one chance in one thousand of ending up in jail for refusing induction. Of course those statistics don't mean a thing if you are that one guy in a thousand.

The government simply cannot win a court case where a person files a valid CO claim, is determined enough to use up all of his appeal rights attempting to get the claim granted, and then follows through by refusing induction. If anything, his refusal is further proof of his sincere conscientious objection to going into the military. In many such cases the US Attorney (the prosecutor) will review the case, decline prosecution, and send the file back to the local board with a recommendation that they "reconsider" it in light of the new evidence of sincerity - the fact that the man refused induction and risked prosecution rather than violate his beliefs.

Some people have refused induction on the grounds of a denied 1-O claim, and shortly thereafter have received a new classification from their local board. In many cases it has been the 1-O which they requested, but in a few cases it was a new 1-A classification. In either case it means the US Attorney declined prosecution. If the new classification is a 1-A, the objector should be sure to request his personal appearance and appeal rights all over again. (See Chapters 11, 12 and 13.) If you find yourself in this situation, you should have little trouble getting your 1-O granted the second time around, although it has occasionally happened that an objector has had to refuse induction several times before the SS finally understood that he was sincere in his beliefs and was not going into the military.

During past drafts, very few people who refused induction because of a denied CO claim were sent to jail.[23] However, there is always the danger of being charged with violations other than refusing induction. For instance, a person could be in a situation where he could be charged with refusing induction **and** failure to keep the SS informed of a current address, or perhaps late registration. Being charged with two or more counts was used frequently during the Vietnam draft. A conviction on **any** count carries the same five year/$10,000 maximum penalty. People considering refusing inducion would be well advised to keep their records clean of all other potential charges, and to have an experienced draft lawyer look over their files prior to the refusal.

For the potential conscientious objector who is convicted in court, an average sentence in the past has been three years of summary probation along with a mandatory two years alternate service work.[24] Since the two run at the same time (concurrently) the whole thing comes out to three years of sending in forms swearing that you have not been caught breaking the law, two years of which must be spent doing alternate service work. But as mentioned earlier, the objector convicted of refusing a **work order** stands a much stronger chance of being sentenced to prison.

The possibility of a prison term, however slim a possibility, along with the fear of being convicted of a felony, seems to scare a lot of people into accepting induction against their judgment. There is an alternative.

An objector who decides not to risk a prison sentence by refusing induction can still have the courts review the SS action on his CO claim by **accepting** induction and having his lawyer file what is known as a Habeas Corpus Petition in federal court. Under that system, the court will review the induction order to see if it was legal, including a review of whether the CO claim was legally turned down. The review generally takes only a week or two, and if the judge agrees that you should not have been drafted, he or she will order the military to **immediately** release you. The problem, of course, is that if the judge feels that the CO claim was properly denied, you are stuck in the military. On the other hand, if you refuse induction you are taking a chance on being convicted and possibly going to jail - particularly if there are other charges that could be brought against you in addition to the charge of refusing induction. Neither alternative is terribly appealing, but at least there are alternatives to choose from. And, for the person who decides to accept induction and whose Habeas Corpus Petition is denied in a court under civil law, there is still the possibility that a counselor or lawyer experienced in **military** law may be able to assist in obtaining a discharge in a military proceeding.

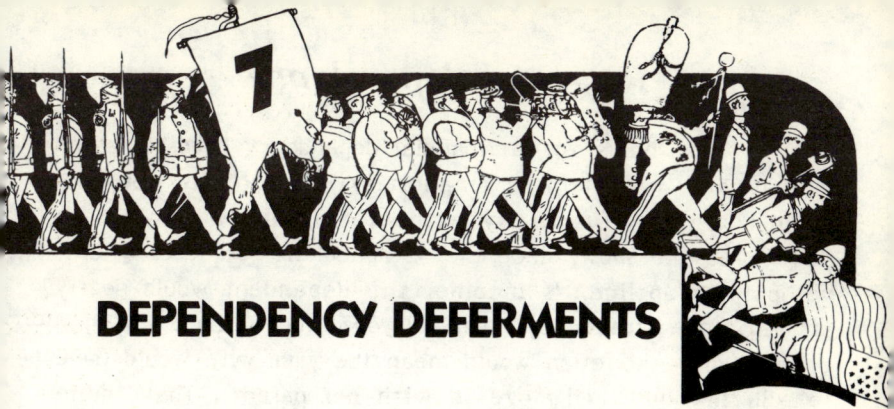

DEPENDENCY DEFERMENTS

If you can show that your induction would cause a hardship to someone who is your dependent, you may be eligible for a dependency deferment (Classification 3-A).[1] Draft regulations say that the term "dependent" means a member of one's close family - wife, child, brother, sister, parent or grandparent.[2] While there are situations where other people, such as uncles, cousins, or "live-in friends" may be dependent upon a draft registrant, the regulations do not allow deferment for men in those situations. Of course, one can always apply and try to convince the local board to bend the rules. But getting them to do so is likely to be rough.

In all claims for 3-A status you must show that your being drafted would cause a hardship for your dependent. Where the dependent is your wife, however, you must show more: you must show that your induction would cause an **extreme** hardship.[3]

There are different kinds of hardship claims: financial hardship, physical hardship, and emotional or psychological hardship. All three are covered by classification 3-A. In the past the most common dependency claim has been based on financial hardship. The form used by the SS (Dependency Questionnaire, Form 118) reflects the predominance of financial dependency claims in that most of the questions on the form are concerned with money and financial affairs.

Financial dependency

The basis for a financial dependency hardship claim is that your dependent is financially supported by you, and could not get by financially without your income.[4] This is never easy to show, since the SS is looking for cases where, without the applicant's income, the dependent would nearly starve in the streets. By no means does the SS care whether or not your induction would mean the your wife would have to sell the house and move in with her parents. That's quite all right with them, as long as she would have a place to stay and food to eat.

Generally, you must show that if you were drafted, your dependent would have absolutely no one to turn to for help. That doesn't mean that no one is available to help, but that anyone the SS might consider "available" would in fact refuse or not be able to help. For instance, you need not show that your parents cannot afford to support your wife (although that would make a fine claim). It is enough to show that your parents don't like your wife and would **refuse** to assist her financially, even if they had ten million dollars in the bank.

Taking the example a little further, you would also have to show that in addition to having no one to turn to, you and your wife don't have enough in savings or investments for her to get by, that she can not work to support herself, and that even figuring in Welfare and other sources of income, she would not be able to make it. When the SS says extreme hardship, they mean **extreme.** As difficult as it may be to prove all of those things, it has been done successfully by many people, so you shouldn't lose hope.

Because of raises in military pay, military dependency allotments have also been raised. In that way financial dependency claims have become more difficult to prove. Still, considering what the military pays a new draftee, someone who is barely scraping by on civilian wages will probably be able to make out a valid claim for deferment. A person doesn't have to be destitute and in hock up to his ears to qualify. But it helps.

Physical dependency

The second type of hardship claim is that of physical dependency. While this is a rarely claimed deferment, it is probably one of the easiest to get granted, provided that one qualifies for it. In order to qualify, you must be able to show that someone is physically dependent upon you, and that there is no one else who could take your place if you were drafted.

For instance, if Johnny's only blood relative is his mother, and she is crippled and needs him to help her to survive, he may be on his way. Here again we may run into the money game. Considering Mom's Social Security money and any savings she may have, why can't Mom afford to live in a convalescent home? Can she afford a live-in nurse or other hired help to do the tasks which she has relied upon her son to do? The SS isn't going to much care that Mom would prefer to have Johnny around doing them, as long as they feel that someone would take care of her.

Let's look at another situation. Let's say that Paul's living relations are his mother and his retarded brother. His mother can get along by herself all right, but she has to work to support Paul and his brother. While Paul does hold a night job and helps out financially, his real claim may be in the fact that he has to be around during the day to care for his brother while his mother is at work.

Of course, the situations discussed here don't begin to exhaust all of the possibilities. There are some cases where the person claiming physical dependency doesn't even

live with his dependent, but still qualifies for the 3-A deferment. The best way to evaluate a situation is to discuss it with a draft counselor. One good rule of thumb is for you to file if you feel that you **might** qualify. The worst that could happen is that the claim will be denied by the local board.

Emotional dependency

The third type of hardship claim is based on emotional dependency. This seems to be a largely overlooked source of deferment, especially for married people and those who come from very close-knit families. In order to get an emotional hardship claim granted, you must show that your dependent is emotionally needful of having you around, and that if you were drafted it would cause the dependent extreme mental anguish and possibly result in psychiatric problems.

Naturally, most potential draftees have family or friends who don't want to see them drafted. But a draft board is unlikely to be sympathetic to a sobbing mother claiming that she couldn't sleep nights if her sweet little darling got drafted. Once again, the key word to remember is not inconvenience, but **hardship.**

A dependent with a past history of psychiatric care makes for a much stronger claim, but that is not absolutely necessary. Nor is it necessary to prove beyond a doubt that a dependent would suffer a complete break-down without you around. The point to make is that it very well could happen, not that it positively would. The important thing is not "proof beyond a reasonable doubt", but enough proof to convince a local board to grant a deferment.

As with a physical hardship claim, you are going to have to work around the traditional Dependency Questionnaire and rely on statements rather than financial resumes to carry the claim. In an emotional hardship claim, a report from a psychiatrist or psychologist concerning the dependent's state of mind is almost mandatory. In cases like that, a sympathetic psychiatrist or psychologist can be extremely helpful.

Filing for 3-A

The process of filing for a hardship deferment is relatively simple. The claim may be prepared on a Dependency Questionnaire (SS Form 118) or can simply be documented along those same lines without using the form. The claim may be based upon any of the three kinds of hardship discussed above, or any combination of the three. For instance, if your dependent is both emotionally unstable and depends on your income, both kinds of dependency should be documented for presentation to the board. Let them decide which basis to use for granting the 3-A, but be sure to give them as many realistic options as possible.

In terms of documentation, probably the most important things will be: 1) A statement explaining the nature of the dependency and pointing out why your being drafted will cause a hardship, along with a similar statement from the dependent. 2) If financial dependency is involved, you should work out family budgets that show both the current cash flow situation and how things would change if you were drafted. If you use SS Form 118, you should be sure not to limit yourself to the tiny spaces provided on the form. 3) You should get statements from others who can verify that the claimed situation exists. This might include doctors, psychiatrists, social workers, ministers, friends, relatives, neighbors, or anyone else familiar with the situation. The letters should be addressed to the local board, or "To whom it may concern," but should be given directly to you and **not** sent to the SS. You will want to go over the letters with your counselor before submitting them, and will want to make copies for your own files as well.

As with other claims for deferment or exemption, no one will be allowed to submit a claim until drafting actually begins. However, a man who feels qualified for a 3-A deferment can take advantage of that fact by starting **now** to gather the needed documentation. The claim may require a bit of updating before being submitted at some future date, but at least the majority of the work will be done.

If and when inductions begin and the claim is submitted, the local board may offer you the opportunity to discuss your claim with them before they decide on your classification.[5] This is called a pre-classification interview. For a further explanation of this process see Chapter 13. A man requesting a dependency deferment has the right to appear before the local board either before or after an initial classification decision is made, but not both. In my opinion the better tactic is to decline the pre-classification interview and allow the board to decide on the basis of the written information submitted. However, you may wish to consult with a draft counselor familiar with the board in question before making this decision.

Once a claim is submitted to the local board, it will consider the claim at its next scheduled meeting and decide whether or not to grant the request for a 3-A deferment. If a pre-classification interview has been requested, you will be given at least fifteen days advance notice of the date that the local board intends to consider the claim.[6] If you choose not to have a pre-classification interview the board will consider the claim without you and decide on its own. They will notify you of their decision by mail.

If you are notified that your new classification is 3-A, it means that the board has accepted your claim and has granted the hardship deferment. Be aware that a 3-A classificaton is only a deferment, not an exemption. That means that it is not permanent, and that you will need to re-document the claim from time to time, at least once a year.[7] So don't lose track of your draft counselor, your doctor, or others who have assisted you.

On the other hand, you may be notified by the local board that, based on information submitted, they do not feel justified in granting you a 3-A deferment. That does not mean that your claim has been shot down forever, but only that you are going to have to work a bit to try to get it granted. You will have full appeal rights at this point (see Chapters 11, 12 and 13) and should get together with your draft counselor to discuss further action.

As discussed in Chapter 12, you have the right to present at least three witnesses at your local board hearing, regardless of whether it is a pre-classification interview or a post-classification hearing. I strongly recommend that in hardship cases one of your witnesses be your dependent. If a doctor is involved, he or she should also be asked to appear. They are the people best qualified to discuss the claim with the board. In any event, dependency is sometimes difficult to prove to a board, and the help of an experienced draft counselor is highly recommended for anyone considering a 3-A deferment.

SURVIVING SONS

There is a popular misconception that if you are the only male in your family who can carry on the family name you can not be drafted. This just isn't true. The purpose of the surviving son or sole surviving son exemption (4-G) is not to assure perpetuation of the family name, but to limit the number of deaths or disabilities in any one family as a result of service in the United States military.[1]

The 4-G classification actually covers two classes of people: "surviving sons" and "sole surviving sons". Both groups are given a draft exemption,[2] meaning that once a draft-age man receives a 4-G classification he can never be re-evaluated for the draft. However, if his entitlement to the 4-G should change, or if the availability of a 4-G exemption were eliminated, he could then be subject to the draft.

Neither class of 4-G exemption is easy to get, and the mere fact that such exemptions exist point up the fact that every generation of United States citizens has been forced into war and suffered casualties for nearly the entire history of our country.

Sole surviving son

To qualify for exemption as a sole surviving son one must meet two requirements.[3] First, your father, brother or sister must have been killed in action, died in the line of duty, or died as a result of injuries or disease incurred while serving in a branch of the United States military. No one seems to know why, but for some reason you are **theoretically** not qualified for a 4-G if your **mother** died as a result of military service. Should you be in that situation, I strongly urge you to file for a 4-G exemption and, if necessary, challenge that aspect of the law. In the past, some local boards have recognized such claims despite the wording of the law.

The second requirement for a sole surviving son exemption is that you must be the only living son of your father. A man who otherwise qualifies, but whose mother later re-married and had other sons, should still qualify for exemption as a sole surviving son.[4]

Surviving sons

Even if you have living brothers, you may qualify for exemption as a surviving son.[5] To qualify under this class you must show that your father, brother or sister was killed in action or died in the line of duty while serving in the United States military, and that they died after December 31, 1959. You can also qualify if your father, brother or sister died after that date as a result of injuries or disease incurred while in the military. The important thing is the **date of death**, not the dates of service. If your father received injuries during the Korean war, and those injuries caused his death in 1965, you should qualify. Note that the death of a **mother** theoretically will not suffice for exemption as a 4-G surviving son. But, once again, people in that situation should still file.

There is also a surviving son deferment (not an exemption) for anyone whose father, brother or sister is presently captured or missing in action as a result of military service.[6] In this situation the 4-G classification would end if the captured or missing family member were to return alive.

General provisions

The 4-G exemption for sole surviving sons and surviving sons will keep you from being drafted into the military or into civilian alternate service work **except** during a Congressionally declared war or national emergency.[7] Bear in mind that **Congress** has not declared a war since 1941 (although the United States has had a couple of undeclared wars since then). Also note that the "national emergency" declared during the Vietnam war was declared by the President, not by Congress, and so the 4-G exemption was still available.

There is no requirement that a man qualified for a 4-G exemption live with or support the surviving family members. If you do, you may also qualify for deferment with a 3-A classification. (See Chapter 7.) But the Supreme Court has said that the purpose of the 4-G exemption is not only to provide "solace and consolation" to the remaining family members, but also to "avoid extinguishing the male line of a family" by allowing "the death in action of the only surviving son," and to allow "fairness to the registrant who has lost his father" as a result of military service.[8]

One qualified for a 4-G exemption should gather documents to prove it. If you are receiving survivors' benefits, copies of all documents submitted to the Veterans Administration should be obtained. If those are not available, a copy of a death-notification letter or telegram, or a sworn statement from another family member may help. In short, you need to prove to the SS that a member of your immediate family has died as a result of being in the military.

If the family member died after leaving the military, but death was caused by an illness or injury incurred while in the military, you may run into problems in trying to prove the cause of death, or in trying to document that the illness or injury causing death was incurred during military service. Military medical and personnel records can be obtained under the Freedom of Information Act from the Military Personnel Records Center, 9700 Page Boulevard, Saint Louis, MO 63132. A local veterans' group may also be of assistance. If a doctor treated the deceased family member for his or her terminal illness, the doctor may be able to verify the actual cause of death, and tie it to the military-incurred disease or injury.

As with all other deferments and exemptions, it is up to the area office or local draft board to decide whether an applicant is qualified for a 4-G exemption. If a claim for exemption is denied, the appeals process discussed in Chapters 12 and 13 should be used.

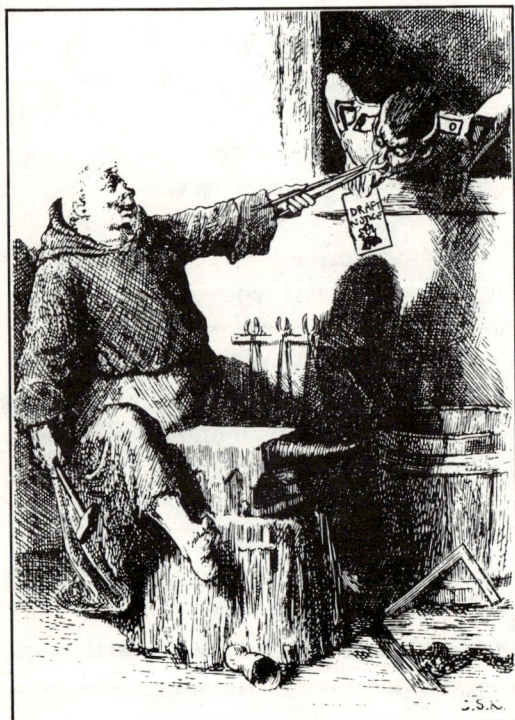

MINISTERS AND MINISTERIAL STUDENTS

The draft law provides complete draft exemption for practicing ministers of religion, with a 4-D exemption.[1] It also provides a student deferment for theological or pre-theological students, with a 2-D deferment.[2] These facts have given rise to a popular misconception that merely being a minister will keep a person from being drafted. Unfortunately it isn't quite that easy.

Ministers

The law exempts both "duly ordained" and "regular" ministers who regularly act as ministers of religion.[3] Apparently the reason for exempting both "duly ordained" and "regular" ministers is to allow the leaders of both formal and informal religious organizations to qualify. In other words, a minister need not be formally ordained to qualify, so long as the ministry is his vocation. But any minister, ordained or not, will qualify for a 4-D exemption only if he is practicing his ministry on a full time or regular basis.[4] This is referred to as the "vocation" requirement.

The vocation requirement for ministerial exemption demands that the ministry must be a man's chief concern. He must engage in ministerial duties regularly, and be recognized by his congregation as a leader or minister of the group. Merely being ordained, be it by a recognized church or by a group which will "ordain" anyone for five or ten dollars, is not enough.

The vocation requirement does not mean that a minister may not hold a secular job, or work outside his ministry.[5] Most courts reviewing the question have tended to look more toward the importance of a man's activities rather than the amounts of time spent pursuing them, or the formal title given him.[6] However, at least one court has said that local boards may properly consider whether a man spends at least half his time on ministerial duties. The real point seems to be that a 4-D exemption should be given to anyone who is actually acting as a minister. If he must also work at a secular job to support himself or his family, he can still qualify if he shows that the ministry is his main concern and vocation, and that his secular job is secondary to it.

If a minister must hold a secular job because his church, sect or organization can not support him, he should be prepared to submit evidence of that, such as a letter from a superior explaining the situation. If he is taking courses or studying on his own to increase his effectiveness as a minister, proof of that should also be secured. Letters from officers of the denomination or congregation should also be gathered. Those letters should point out his importance to the congregation, as well as emphasizing that he does have a true ministry and a community of faith which he serves.

Difficulties with gaining a 4-D exemption often arise when the ministry is other than "traditional" in nature. Jehovah's Witnesses often encounter problems gaining 4-D exemption, as do "street ministers" or others lacking a well defined "congregation". In such cases it must be shown that the minister serves a community of faith in much the same way a minister with a more traditional congregation serves his community of faith. The real issue here is whether the applicant teaches and preaches the principles of faith and regularly conducts some kind of services for the community to which he is ministering.

The SS may not deny a 4-D exemption to a minister solely on the basis that he has not had sufficient preparation for the ministry or because he has not attended a theological school.[7]

Theology students

Men who attend a theological school and are not yet ministers are entitled to a 2-D student deferment. To qualify for the deferment you must show that you are preparing for the ministry under the direction of a "recognized" church or religious organization, and that you are satisfactorily pursuing a full-time course of instruction in a "recognized" theological or divinity school.[8] A "recognized" theological or divinity school means one with an established reputation, and whose curriculum and academic standards will be acceptable to the church or religious organization sponsoring the student. A "recognized" church or religious organization is defined as one which was established on the basis of a community of faith and belief, and which engages primarily in religious activities. Obviously, if either the school or the church is not well known, and particularly if its practices might not be seen as "religious" by a local board, problems may arise. For instance, courts have said that a group of people who gather together each week to eat peyote buttons and experience nature are not a "church".

A 2-D student deferment is also available to pre-theology students. To qualify you must show that you are preparing for the ministry under the direction of a "recognized" church or religious organization, that you have been pre-enrolled by a "recognized" theological or divinity school, and that you are satisfactorily pursuing a full time course of instruction required for entrance into the theological school in which you are pre-enrolled.

The 2-D lasts only as long as you continue to meet all of the requirements. Should you complete your education and become a minister, you may or may not qualify for exemption as a minister. On the other hand, if you discontinue your course of study, or if the local board feels that your academic progress is not "satisfactory", the deferment could be withdrawn.

"Satisfactory progress" has been defined to mean that during the academic year a man has earned a full proportion of credits toward his degree, enough to complete his degree in the normal time for that program. This means that a student in a four year school must earn **at least** 25% of the credits required for graduation in **each** of his years of study.

A man qualified for a 2-D deferment should gather documents showing his enrollment or pre-enrollment in a school of theology or divinity, and should be prepared to submit proof in support of his claim, such as letters from the school registrar verifying his enrollment, showing his grades, and discussing his rate of progress.

MEDICAL SPECIALIST AND MEDICAL STUDENTS

Special provisions of the draft law allow the SS to conduct a special draft for doctors and registered nurses.[1] Since most of the people subject to this special draft are doctors, it will be referred to as the doctors' draft, and references will be to doctors rather than doctors and nurses, but you registered nurses must remember to include yourselves.

Rather than being put into the usual priority groups and drafted (see Chapter 2), doctors are kept apart from everyone else.[2] When the military needs doctors it sends out a special call for a certain number of them, itemized by specialty.[3] For instance, there might be a draft for 317 Medical Doctors, 167 Dentists, 52 Osteopaths, and so on. There could be one or more doctors drafts each year, or several years could pass with no doctors being drafted. A doctors' draft could be limited to one class of medical specialist, or could include virtually every field. It all depends on what the military decides it wants.

When doctors are drafted they are given an option. They can accept induction as a regular Private, or they can agree to enter the military as an officer, to practice medicine. Needless to say, few doctors who go into the military choose to do so as Privates. So in effect the purpose of a doctors' draft is not really to **draft** doctors, but to coerce them into accepting an officer's commission and entering the military as a medical specialist.

Many doctors have their education subsidized or paid for by the military, in exchange for an agreement to serve in the military as a doctor after internship or residency. These people are classified as military reservists. They are members of the military, and are subject to the laws of the military, not the SS. Doctors seeking to avoid such an obligation should consult a counselor or lawyer experienced in that field of **military law**, and should not rely on the **draft law** informaton in this book.

You may be wondering how doctors ever get drafted, since there aren't many twenty-year-old doctors around, and the First Priority Group is traditionally comprised mainly of twenty-year-olds. The draft law says that anyone who has ever received a draft deferment can be drafted until age thirty-five. While this "extended liability" is not generally used, doctors are one group to whom it is commonly applied, and they are therefore eligible to be drafted until they reach thirty-five.

Order of call

The Order of Call for doctors is similar to the regular Order of Call discussed in Chapter 2. Doctors are drafted out of Priority Groups in lottery number order. The classifications indicating a doctor's availability to be drafted include the two conscientious objector classifications as well as the "fully available" 1-A classification,[4] with the variation that a 1-A medical specialist is classified 1-AM. Within the 1-AM classification, medical specialists are further classified by specialty. Medical doctors qualified for induction are classified 1-AMM, dentists are 1-AMD, optometrists are classified 1-AME, osteopaths are 1-AMO, podiatrists are 1-AMP, veterinarians are 1-AMV, and registered nurses are 1-AMN. If a call went out to draft dentists, for example, those dentists classified 1-AMD would be subject to being drafted.

The Priority Groups for medical specialists are defined according to when the specialist attains the **first** appropriate professional degree or diploma, **or** upon completion of internship or one year of equivalent training, whichever is **later.**[5] The internship or equivalent training must immediately follow receipt of a professional degree.[6]

A medical specialist is put into the doctors' Fisrt Priority Group during the year immediately following receipt of his professional degree or completion of his internship, whichever is later.[7] For instance, a doctor who completed his internship on June 30 would be placed in the doctors' First Priority Group through June 29 of the following year. In other words, doctors' Priority Groups are **not** based on **calendar** years, but **actual** years since completion of training. After spending a year in First Priority a doctor drops into the doctors' Second Priority Group for one year, then into the Third Priority Group, and so on.

Reaching Second Priority or some lower priority group is no assurance that a doctor will face a decreased likelihood of being drafted. To the contrary, the military's demand for medical specialists is so great that most doctors can virtually count on being subject to a special call at least once before reaching age 35. Naturally, being called does not automatically mean that a doctor will be **inducted.** But with the strong possibility of being subject to a call, doctors are well advised to be prepared if they wish to avoid induction or coerced commissioning as an officer.

Calls from each Priority Group must be in lottery number order,[8] and all specialists in that field must be called from the First Priority Group before anyone in that field may be called from the Second Priority Group.[9] But bear in mind that calls are by specialty, so that a call for dentists might be filled from First Priority while a call for medical doctors made at the same time could dip into Third Priority.

Alien doctors (non-US citizens) enter First Priority in the same manner as US citizens, with the exception that aliens who are **already** doctors when they enter the United States as permanent residents are entitled to a 4-C classification for their first year of residence in the US. (See Appendix A for further information concerning aliens.)

Deferment or exemption

Subject to certain differences, doctors are eligible for the same deferments and exemptions available to other draft registrants. One of the notable differences is that doctors may qualify for deferment on the basis that their services are needed in their community. This is known as the "community essentiality" deferment, available only to doctors, and is represented by a classification of 2-AM.[10] To qualify for a 2-AM deferment a doctor must show that the work he is doing is essential to the community in which he works, and that if he were drafted he could not be replaced. A 2-AM deferment is most likely to be given to a doctor working in a small community, doctors with special skills, and those working in free clinics or impoverished areas. Bear in mind that a doctor must be **irreplaceable** to qualify for a 2-AM. The regulations also state that a doctor in the doctors' First Priority Group **is not eligible** for a 2-AM deferment. It is usually best for a doctor seeking a 2-AM to gather letters from his peers and superiors to show why his being drafted would create or aggravate a lack of medical care in the community, and that his services could not be replaced if he were drafted.

Another difference for doctors involves the 1-A-OM conscientious objector classification. (See Chapter 6.) Since a 1-A-O objects only to combatant duty, a doctor filing for a 1-A-OM would accomplish little. As a 1-A-OM or as a 1-AM, he would still most likely end up in the same non-combatant status: the medical corps. While doctors can certainly qualify for 1-A-OM status, doing so seems an exercise in futility. It would, of course, guarantee that the doctor would not be assigned a combatant role. But by and large, trained medical personnel are too valuable to the military to be used in that capacity anyway. However, conscientious objector doctors may get 1-OM status, and in that event would be called to perform civilian alternate service work, rather than military duty, if he would otherwise have been inducted as a 1-AM.[11]

Another important difference for doctors involves the 4-FM exemption. Unlike other draftees, doctors are evaluated under a different and far less stringent set of medical standards.[12] A man qualified for a 4-F exemption as a regular draftee may nonetheless be found fully qualified for induction as a doctor. Furthermore, men previously given a 4-F exemption while subject to the regular draft can be re-examined under the medical standards for doctors, and of course could be found qualified. If a doctor cannot pass the medical standard's for doctors, he will be given a 4-FM exemption.

Sliding by a special call

Special calls for doctors are made for a limited period of time. For instance, a call might go out for a certain number of medical specialists from stated fields of training to be inducted during a given six month period. In most cases a special call will last only for a period of months, and any doctors not actually inducted or otherwise pressed into military service will not be called after the close of the special call. . . until another special call is made. Because of the limited nature of special calls, it may be possible for a doctor to avoid being inducted simply by not being eligible for the duration of the special call.

Naturally, the most obvious way for a doctor to not be eligible during a special call is for him to be deferred or exempted. But doctors should also bear in mind that a man can not be inducted while he is appealing his classification, or while his period of time in which to appeal is still running.

For instance, let's say that Daniel Crone is currently classified (or presumed classified) 1-AMM and has been placed in the First Priority Group for doctors. He learns through his draft counselor that a special call for medical doctors will be held from March 1 through May 31. On February 26 Dr. Crone submits information to his local board that he is a conscientious objector, that he qualifies for a community essentiality deferment, or that he is in some other way qualified for a deferment or exemption other than a 4-F medical exemption.

Upon receipt of the information from Dr. Crone, the local board is required to re-open his classification and consider him for the classification he is requesting. Regardless of whether the classification he asks for is ultimately granted or denied, the chances are quite good that by the time Dr. Crone has completely used up all of his rights to appeal, the special call period will have passed. If it has passed, Dr. Crone can no longer be called, even if his claim for deferment or exemption was denied, since the legal authority to call him (the special call) will have elapsed. For more information on appealing as a stall tactic, see Chapters 11, 12 and 13.

Medical students

A 2-M draft deferment is available to men who are satisfactorily pursuing a medical education.[13] To qualify, you must actually be enrolled in a medical school - a pre-med course of study is not enough. By accepting a 2-M student deferment, you will most likely be extending your draft liability to age thirty-five under the doctors' draft. By refusing it, you take a chance on being drafted long before you complete your education.

The 2-M student deferment is available to those enrolled in a course of study leading to a degree as a medical doctor, dentist, optometrist, osteopath, podiatrist, veterinarian, or registered nurse. To apply for a 2-A, you should be prepared to provide proof of your student status and your course of study, and to show that you are making "satisfactory progress" toward receipt of a degree as a medical specialist.

"Satisfactory progress" means that each year a man must earn sufficient credits to constitute the same proportion of the credits needed to obtain a degree as the years of his completed schooling bear to the total time needed to be awarded the degree. In other words, a man enrolled in a four year course of study for which 120 credits are needed must earn at least 30 credits each year, since each year represents 25% of the time needed, and 30 credits represents 25% of the credits needed.

Records from college counselors and registrars should be gathered, showing that you are enrolled in a full-time course of study, and that your progress is at least average.

If you discontinue your medical course of study, or if your grades or rate of progress become "unsatisfactory" in the eyes of your local board, your deferment will be discontinued. You could then be subject to the draft as a regular draftee.

HOW TO DEAL WITH A DISAGREEABLE CLASSIFICATION

The most important thing for you to know about classification is that almost any time you are sent a new classification you have a legal right to question it.[1] The process of questioning it is commonly known as "appealing the classification." Appealing gives you a chance to have your classification changed and also keeps you from being drafted - at least for a while. You cannot be inducted while you are appealing your classification.[2]

The procedures described in this book are current as of the date of publication, but like all laws, they are subject to change. If you are going to act upon this information, it is essential that you check to see if there have been changes. First, make sure that you have the most current edition of this book, then check with a draft counselor or lawyer.

The appeal process

There are three steps involved in the appeal process: the local board personal appearance, the state appeal, and the national appeal.

The first step, the local board personal appearance, may be offered to you before you are classified in the form of a "pre-classification interview" with the local board. Anyone who has filed for a 1-A-O, 1-O or 3-A classificaton must be offered the opportunity to appear in person in front of his local board, either before it decides his classification or afterward, but not both.[3]

At the local board personal appearance you will have the chance to come face to face with the members of your local board. This may be the only time in your life that you can actually meet the people who are trying to send you off to the military. You can ask the board members why they gave you your particular classification. You can ask them if there has been a mistake in your classification. You can ask them why they don't volunteer to go in your place. More importantly, you can show them why you feel that your classification is wrong, and why you feel qualified for a different one.

Why you should appeal

Many draft registrants wonder why they should bother to appeal. Their feeling seems to be that they are likely to be drafted eventually, so why prolong things?

It may very well be that you will eventually be drafted, but here are two facts from the Vietnam draft for you to think about:
* More than 180,000 men avoided the draft in early 1972, and they had one thing in common: they had all stalled off their induction, either by appealing or by other methods.
* Most changes in classfication came about as a direct result of a local board personal appearance.

Even if your classification is not changed as a result of appealing, you are no worse off. In fact, you are probably much better off in four important ways: First, you have let the SS know that you are not happy about the classification you have been given. Second, you have been in a state of appeal, which could make the difference between being drafted and not. Third, if you have submitted any evidence to show why you should have a different classification, you have built up a file, and this can make a **very** big difference in the eventual outcome of your case. Fourth, you have forced the draft board to take some kind of legal action. This means they have to justify not changing your classification, and also justify giving you that classification in the first place. This gives the SS more chances to screw up something, and believe me, they are a bureaucracy, and they are good at screwing things up. It happens very often. Such mistakes, known as "procedural errors," can make a great difference in your processing.

I believe that one should almost always appeal any classification they don't want.

How to appeal

You have the right to appeal any time you are given a new or different classification.[4] You may appeal directly to an appeal board,[5] but by doing so you give up the right to a local board personal appearance. There are very strict rules governing what you have to do and, especialy, when you have to do it in order to use this right.

You **must** be aware of the strict time limit. Under current regulations you are allowed only fifteen days from the **mailing date** of your new classification in which to request the first step in the appeal process - the local board personal appearance. This time limit is one of the things that may get changed, but at present, considering that mail can take a long time to get delivered, you can see the urgency for your being completely prepared and in touch with your mailbox.

It bears repeating: in order to appeal your classification you must request a local board personal appearance or an appeal to the appeal board within fifteen days from the mailing date of your new classification. For instance, if a classification was assigned by a local board at its meeting on August 1, but was mailed out to you on August 10, you have until August 25 to request a local board personal appearance or an appeal. The request does not have to be in the hands of the local board by August 25, but it must be **post-marked** not later than midnight on August 25.

The request should be in writing, and can be in the form of a letter to the local board. It should contain your name in type or print, the date, your SS number, and your signature. The letter can be lengthy or it can be short and to the point. About all you need to say is, "I request a personal appearance with the local board to discuss my classification." You can say more if you wish, but you don't have to. It is a good idea to avoid using the word "appeal", since that may be interpreted by the local board clerk to mean that you are requesting a state appeal and giving up your right to a local board personal appearance.

Communicating with the SS

This is a good time to bring up a few points about communications with the SS. I have already mentioned the importance of keeping a copy of your registration form, and having proof that you registered on time. Any further communications with the SS, including any changes of address, should **always** be in writing and should be sent by **certified mail, return receipt requested.** You should also keep at least one photocopy of **everything** that you send the SS, and should keep **everything** that they send to you.

No, I don't work for the Post Office or own a lot of Xerox stock. There are some good, practical reasons for these suggestions, as illustrated in the examples below.

Let's say that Steve Huston receives a 1-A and goes down to his local board to request a personal appearance.

What proof does he have of having requested it? None! Even if he presents his request in writing, what if the local board clerk "loses" his request? What if, two weeks later, the clerk denies ever having seen Steve? Steve is in trouble!

If Steve had sent his request by **certified mail, return receipt requested,** he would have legal proof of who at the SS office received it. If he also kept a photocopy of his request, he would have legal proof of just what it was that he had mailed. Without that proof, he may be denied the right to a local board personal appearance and to an appeal of his classification.

Let's take another example. Let's say that Chuck Liebling got a very low lottery number and is ordered to report for induction. Along with the order for induction he also receives a questionnaire asking, among other things, whether he is a conscientious objector. Chuck immediately fills out the form to indicate that he is a conscientious objector and mails it off to the SS. However, somewhere between his local post office and the SS office, the letter is lost.

A few weeks pass, and Chuck begins to wonder what has become of his request to be classified as a conscientious objector. He contacts his local board, and is told that no such request was ever received, that he failed to report for induction as ordered, and that his file has been turned over to the United States Attorney's office for prosecution. If Chuck had used certified mail, return receipt requested, and kept a copy of the form, his lawyer would have no trouble getting the charges dropped and forcing Chuck's local board to hear his conscientious objector claim. As it is, Chuck may very well be prosecuted, convicted, and sent to prison.

Certified mail, return receipt requested, involves the use of two Post Office forms. The first, the certification receipt, is date-stamped at the Post Office at the time of mailing. It provides proof of the date of mailing, and also shows the address to which the letter was mailed. It should be immediately clipped or stapled to the photocopy of the letter and put somewhere safe, where it won't get lost or eaten by your kid brother. The return receipt is a little card which you address to yourself. It is attached to the letter that you are mailing, and the certification number is recorded on it. When the postal person delivers the letter, the addressee (the SS) has to sign for the letter. The return receipt is then removed from the letter, date stamped, and mailed back to the sender. It is your legal proof that the SS got the letter, when it was received, and who received it. The return receipt should be attached to the photocopy of the letter and kept in your file.

In order to send mail certified, return receipt, it is necessary to get window service at the Post Office. Be sure to bear this in mind when calculating deadlines. For example, if you are requesting a local board personal appearance, and your fifteenth day falls on a weekend, you will have to mail your request the previous Friday. If you wait until Monday, it will be too late.

The law regarding a registrant's communications with the SS is very bad. You are legally responsible for receiving all mail sent to you by the SS, and you are also legally responsible for all of your mail getting to the SS.[6] Apparently the SS just isn't very responsible. There is no real way to insure that everything the SS sends out will get delivered, other than to keep the SS informed of a current mailing address. But there is a way to have proof concerning everything that you send to the SS, so you should make use of it. You should send everything by certified mail, return receipt requested.

The reason for keeping photocopies may not be clear yet. One of these days it just may happen that you will need to have legal proof of something that you sent to the SS.

For example, Steve Huston needed proof that he requested a personal appearance, and Chuck Liebling needed proof that he claimed to be a conscientious objector.

Even people who do not find themselves in such serious circumstances may have many uses for photocopies of the letters they have sent the SS. For example, it is always very helpful to bring a complete copy of your SS file any time you see your draft counselor. Getting a copy of the file from the SS is not impossible, but it is often a giant pain in the rear. Once you finally succeed in convincing the clerk that the SS regulations give you an absolute right to obtain copies of the contents of your file[7] (which may take quite a bit of persuasion) you will be charged twenty-five cents per page for copies.[8] A hand-written copy is not a legally binding copy - it has to be a photocopy or a carbon copy.

If you happen to own a portable photocopy machine, the SS **may** let you use it to copy your file. Then again, they may not. Of course, you can always take your file to a copy machine to make copies. But the SS has the strange notion that if they let everyone borrow their SS files a few of them might not come back, so they send a local board clerk along with men who check out their files. All you have to do is to set up an appointment well in advance, and pay the SS an hourly rate for the services of their clerk.[9]

The bottom line is that it is much easier, faster and cheaper if you make at least one clean photocopy **before** sending anything to the SS, and to save all letters you receive from them. Most libraries have photocopy machines that cost only five to twenty cents per page. Once you have a photocopy made, you should not let go of it - you should always have at least one copy on hand.

You may have noticed that my attitude toward the SS is not trustful. There is good reason for this. Ever heard of the Peter Principle? According to Dr. Peter, people rise to their level of incompetence. As long as a person can handle a job, he continues to be promoted, until promoted to a job that he is incapable of doing. Even though a person may be the best clerk in the office, he may not be up to being a vice-president. In that case, once promoted to vice-president, he will not be recommended for further promotions. Unfortunately, no one will recommend him for a demotion, either. So there he sits for the rest of his life, screwing up a job he can't handle.

The SS is a prime example of the Peter Principle in action, since it is a government bureaucracy. Most local board members have no idea what the SS regulations say; they accept the word of the clerks who are government employees. Most clerks are merely clerks, and no more. If they know anything at all about the SS law, they usually interpret it incorrectly. But that doesn't stop them from answering questions from board members or from registrants. To the contrary, they are more than happy to inform the local board members that it is all right to deny a conscientious objector claim on the ground that a man is not a Quaker, and they are tickled to tell a registrant that he might as well not bother appealing, since he will just get drafted anyway.

This is why I keep stressing that you should not trust these people with your future - unless you don't care about your future.

I am not making these statements simply because I dislike the SS. I have personally dealt with numerous clerks and local board members, and I am not saying that they are all completely ignorant. I am sure that some can even count up to ten, but I certainly wouldn't trust my life to them. Will you?

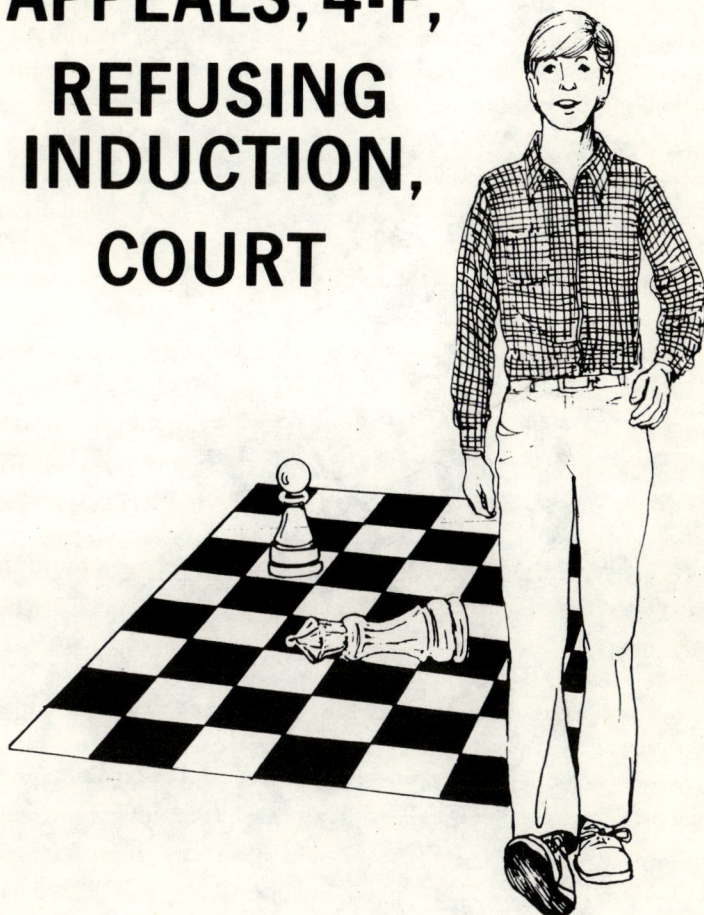

PART THREE: THE END GAMES

APPEALS, 4-F, REFUSING INDUCTION, COURT

THE LOCAL BOARD
PERSONAL APPEARANCE

This chapter is based upon the Selective Service Regulations as they existed during the Vietnam draft. It is possible that new rules will be issued for the next draft call.

Any time you are classified or re-classified (other than receiving a 1-H classification) you have the right to appear in person before your local board to discuss your classification.[1] In cases where you are requesting a Hardship or Conscientious Objector classification, you have the right to appear before your local board either before or after it considers your claim, but not both.[2] If you choose to meet with your local board before it considers your claim, the meeting is known as a "pre-classification interview." If you choose to meet with the board only after it has considered your claim, the meeting is known as a "personal appearance."

There is some disagreement over whether a person would be better off to meet with his local board before or after classification. Some people feel that a pre-classification interview offers the opportunity to appear before board members who have not yet made a decision on the classification, and therefore may be more easily swayed. The argument goes that since the board members have not yet looked for or announced any reason to deny the claim, they may be less defensive and more open to arguments in favor of a claim.

Other people feel that a pre-classification interview will have little, if any, effect on the decision of the local board. They feel that a claim for conscientious objector status or extreme hardship deferment should be strong enough to speak for itself, and that only if it is denied should a person request a personal appearance. An appearance after classification gives the board a chance to grant the requested status without the need for any personal appearance. If the request is denied, the local board must give reasons for denial,[3] and the personal appearance can then be devoted to explaining why you feel the board's reasons for denial are not valid. If you are turned down at a personal appearance, reasons for denial must again be given,[4] and they can once more be refuted at the state appeal level. In effect, requesting a pre-classification interview will cut your appeal rights in half and deny you the right to request the local board to reconsider its decision.

Local draft counselors can probably offer the best advice about whether a pre-classification interview or a post-classification personal appearance seems to sit best with any particular board.

The local board personal appearance will be discussed here as part of the appeal process. If you decide to request a pre-classification interview, the process should be much the same, and most of the information in this chapter should apply.

Information on how and when to request a local board personal appearance is included in Chapter 11. If you haven't read that yet, please do. The most important point to remember is that you must request a personal appearance within the time limit set by the SS, which current regulations say is fifteen days.[5] If you wait any longer, or for some other reason miss the deadline, you have in effect accepted the new classification and given up your right to appeal. While boards can allow "late appeals," they are rarely granted.

Witnesses

You have the right to present witnesses at your personal appearance,[6] and it is strongly recommended you do so. The decision of the local board will be based upon the information in your file at the time of the personal appearance **and** any new information presented at the time of the personal appearance.[7] Presenting witnesses is a very good way to submit new information, especially if you are requesting conscientious objector or hardship status.

The purpose of presenting witnesses is to let the board hear first-hand information from people who know your situation quite well from their own observation and experience. A witness cannot act as legal counsel, which is to say that he or she is not allowed to advise you of your rights.[8] However, there is no reason why your counselor or lawyer cannot testify in your behalf, if the counselor or lawyer is familiar with your claim. Even though the counselor or lawyer will not be allowed to advise you on the spot or act as your legal representative, the counselor or lawyer may be able to assure that a claim is adequately presented to the board, and may also be able to detect procedural errors in the conduct of the meeting which could be used to your advantage later.

You are entitled to present up to three witnesses, but the local board can agree to hear from more than three if it wants to. But local boards are usually not very nice people, so you shouldn't count on having more than three witnesses heard, or any other favors. If you feel that your case would be best presented by using more than three witnesses, you should go ahead and ask the board if it will agree to it. It is always worth a try, but you should be prepared to have your request turned down. Decide ahead of time which three witnesses are most important to your case.

Time is precious. The local board is entitled to cut off an appearance after only fifteen minutes,[9] and that is barely enough time to clear your throat if you are not very well prepared. If each of your three witnesses takes only three minutes, that leaves you only six minutes to present your claim to the board. The law provides that the fifteen minutes may be extended,[10] but you can't count on favors from a local board.

Why appeal?

The kinds of tactics you will want to use at your personal appearance depend upon what your current classification is and what you want to do about it. If you are appealing only as a stall tactic but don't really feel that you are qualified for any other classification, then your tactics will be very different than if you are seriously set upon winning some specific classification, such as conscientious objector status.

One thing should be brought up here. A lot of people may want to appeal their classification because they think they should be classified 4-F. You should be aware that in most cases the local board will not give you a 4-F exemption unless instructed to do so by the AFEES.[11] In other words, you **must** fail an AFEES physical examination before being eligible for a 4-F exemption. Generally speaking, you are not going to get a 4-F exemption as a result of a personal appearance. In fact, the SS may change the regulations to say that you will not be allowed to appeal for a 4-F. However, if such an appeal is allowed, you should go ahead with it. It is certainly better than not appealing at all, and it may focus some attention on your medical claim and do you some good that way. If nothing else, appealing will protect you from an induction order while you work something out medically.

A tactic that has been overlooked by many people is to appeal just for the sake of appealing. Let's say that you have a 1-A classification you don't want, but have no reason to feel qualified for any classification other than 1-A. Obviously, you are unlikely to get any other classification simply by appealing. But then again, you won't get inducted while appealing, and that is worth something. Even though it may not really get you anywhere to appeal, it may still be worth doing.

Some people feel that there is little use in stalling off induction by appealing. They feel that stalling the draft is just putting off the inevitable, and that they will eventually be drafted anyway. There are four thoughts they should consider. First, every day that you stall brings you closer to the magic age of twenty-six when you will no longer be draftable. Second, using appeal rights even as a stall forces the SS to take some kind of action, and gives them an opportunity to commit procedural errors which could result in a benefit to you. Third, it just may be that while appealing you will realize that you are a conscientious objector, or may develop or discover some basis for 4-F exemption or some other deferment or exemption. Last, approximately 180,000 men escaped the draft in March, 1972, with only one thing in common - they had all been stalling.[12] None of those people would have been around to escape the draft if they had not been stalling, some for as long as five years.

If you are appealing as a stall tactic, you might get a kick out of reading sections of the Nuremburg trials to the local board. Or you might want to read them the parts of the United States Constitution which prohibit slavery and indentured servitude. Or maybe just sing the National Anthem and walk out. Another idea is to read the Ten Commandments and then ask the board members why they are drafting people even though a person should not kill and should not covet his neighbor's goods. The board members will likely get embarrassed and terribly defensive in the face of such questions. With a little creative thought, most registrants should be able to come up with all kinds of inspiring ideas. Just a couple words of caution: it is illegal to intentionally disrupt local board business,[13] so you should be sure that you are very clear on how your information affects your draft status. Also, harassment tactics are unlikely to endear you to the local board members, and this should be considered if you may ever request some deferment or exemption from the same local board.

If there is a particular classification you qualify for, it is not recommended that you get too strange with your local board. They just aren't likely to grant your conscientious objector claim if they recall seeing you a few months before under embarrassing circumstances.

Some guidelines

The exact strategy and tactics you will use depends entirely upon your individual situation. This is something you and your counselor can best work out. However, several pointers are offered here which can be useful at almost every local board personal appearance where you are requesting a change of classification. Realize that these are just general practices and not a substitute for competent draft counseling.

Above all, you must stay sober. Yes, sure, you can function better stoned than you can when not stoned, but if you go to your local board appearance all blitzed out, the board will walk all over you. With cleats on. They will chew you up and spit you out, and it will take you a week to figure out what happened. They just aren't very mellow people, and you have to be alert and attentive.

You should find out why your claim was initially turned down by the local board. When the board classified you they were required by law to review everything in your Selective Service file. In truth, they probably didn't, but that is another story. At any rate, if you presented a claim for deferment or exemption the board must have reviewed the claim. If the claim was denied, the board is **required** to give reasons **in writing** for the denial.[14] It may be that those reasons were sent to you along with your classification. If not, you can request them by mail, or you can go to your local board office, ask to see your file, and get a copy of the reasons. If no reasons have been given, you should definitely demand them, pointing out that this procedural error on the part of the board is prejudicial to your rights. That should scare hell out of the clerk, and get you some written reasons in a hurry.

Once you know why the local board denied your claim, you should do your best to show why those reasons are not valid. There are two ways to do this - legally and factually. The board can't turn down a claim just because it doesn't like you or doesn't agree with you. The reasons for turning a claim down must be legal. For instance, a board can not turn down a CO claim because a man has long hair, or doesn't belong to a church. Turning a man down because of the length of his hair is called "personal prejudice", and is not a legal thing for a local board to do.[15] Also, there is no legal requirement that a conscientious objector must belong to a church. In fact, the SS regulations specifically state that a conscientious objector does not have to believe in a God, let alone belong to a church.[16] So that kind of reason is illegal as well.

Factually incorrect reasons are the ones that are not supported by the information in your file. Let's say that the board turns down a conscientious objector application because they feel the applicant is "insincere" in his beliefs (a very common reason given in conscientious objector cases). First, the board must show exactly what information in the man's file leads them to disbelieve his sincerity. If the board cannot show where it got the information causing it to disbelieve a man's sincerity, the reason is probably invalid. The courts have repeatedly held that mere disbelief is not reason enough to deny a conscientious objector claim.[17]

If the local board can show a reason for their denial ("registrant insincere based on evidence of membership in rifle club"), the man's job at the personal appearance will be to show why the board's conclusion is wrong ("although I belong to a rifle club for target shooting, I would never kill a living thing, since living things are a part of God. I certainly would not participate in war in any form.")

Once you know why the board turned down your claim, it would be a good idea for you to discuss their reasons with your draft counselor. Your counselor will be able to tell you whether or not a reason is legal, and will probably have some suggestions on how to best go about showing that the board reached an incorrect conclusion.

You should write up a brief summary of the points you want to make at your personal appearance. It doesn't have to be very long - a page or two is fine, and more than that may be too much. It should be typed, or at least hand-written very neatly and legibly. You should make about six copies. It is fine to use carbon paper for the copies, but the copy you keep in your personal file should be a photocopy. Here's another reminder about your personal file: you should keep everything the SS sends you, and at least one photocopy of everything you submit to the SS. (Be sure to read "Communicating With The SS" in the previous chapter).

Along with your summary, you should outline your main points on an index card, an old envelope, or have them tattooed on your arm. You only need the original copy of these notes.

If at all possible, you should try to find at least one person who can go to the draft board with you as a witness to testify in your behalf. You should ask your witnesses to write up summaries of the points they want to make, and get six copies made for the hearing plus one for your personal file. Witnesses should make notes of their main points, just like you did. Now you are ready for your big day at the SS office.

Courtesy interviews

You will be given at least fifteen days notice of the date for your local board personal appearance.[18] It may happen that you will be scheduled for an appearance at a time when you are far away from your local board and perhaps not able to get back for the appearance. If it is at all humanly possible, you really should make it. If nothing else, making such an effort speaks highly of your sincerity. If you absolutely can't make it, you can try writing to the local board and explaining your problem. You should give them a date when you will be able to appear and request that your personal appearance be rescheduled. The board probably won't change the appearance date, but it is worth a try. If all else fails, or if there is no time when you can appear before your local board, you might want to write them to request a "courtesy interview" with a local board near you. That will allow you to appear before a local board other than your own, and present your case to that local board. The board that hears the claim will then forward the evidence and its recommendations to your local board for a decision.

There are two very real problems with "courtesy interviews." First, your local board need not agree to a courtesy interview, and the other local board does not have to agree to hear you even if your request is approved. If the local board will not allow it, you should curse three times, submit a letter explaining how grossly unfair they are being, and go ahead with the state appeal (Chapter 13).

The second problem with courtesy interviews is that your local board does not have to agree with the results of a courtesy interview. In other words, you could convince the courtesy board to grant you the classification you want, but still get denied by your local board. Nice, no?

As you can see, a courtesy interview is really not a good solution to your problem. If you can make it to your local board personal appearance by any means, that is the best way to go. It just may impress them too. I mean, a man has to be pretty sincere to take off for a few days and travel several hundred miles just to see his draft board, right? Let's hope that the board thinks so, too.

Playing draftboard

A week or so before your personal appearance you may want to get together with several friends, or better yet several draft counselors, and play draft board. It isn't as much fun as playing doctor, but it can help you to get your thoughts together for the actual personal appearance. This process has been found to be very helpful for people who are trying to obtain conscientious objector status, although it is helpful for anyone seeking any deferment or exemption. It often happens that a local board will catch a person unprepared and use the personal appearance to confuse hell out of him. After fifteen minutes of stuttering and stammering, trying to come up with rational answers to irrational questions, a man won't appear too convincing to the local board. They will feel that they are justified in denying the claim, since the man couldn't even answer "simple" questions.

Playing draft board can get you well enough prepared to stand up under the local board's games, no matter what they try to pull. It could also help you to prepare yourself for some of the draft board's ridiculous questions, such as "What would you do if someone were raping your mother?" or "What would you do if God told you to fight a war?" Most draft counselors will have a list of the kinds of questions that draft boards have asked conscientious objector applicants in the past. Those questions may appear senseless, but should be considered. After all, someone else had to deal with being asked those questions, and the local board may enjoy asking them again.

At the personal appearance

By the day of your local board personal appearance you should be well prepared. You should not plan anything for the rest of the day, because you are going to be quite busy.

It is best to show up a bit early for a personal appearance. You will most likely have to wait quite a while before you get in, but if you show up late the board may refuse to see you at all. Take a good book or your knitting. Perhaps a rousing game of pinochle between you and your witnesses might pass the time.

Eventually, you will be called into the local board meeting room. Make sure to glance at a watch or clock and jot down the time of day on the back of your notes. You should bring your summary of important points with you, and have your witnesses bring theirs (all six copies of each). If you have more than three witnesses, you should have copies of their summaries as well. The summaries should **not** be turned in before meeting with the board members. You should keep them in your hot little hand until needed.

The law requires that a majority of the board's members be present.[19] Since a board must have at least three members, and may have up to five,[20] you will be heard by between two and five people.

If you have more than three witnesses you should explain your situation to the board chairperson and ask if the witnesses can testify. Explain why it is necessary to present all of them. You might also want to throw in something

126

about how difficult it was for them to attend the hearing, but that they were willing to do so because they know how important the matter is.

When witnesses are admitted, they should read or paraphrase their summaries, and then hand each board member a copy of the summary, explaining that the summary was written by themselves, not you. The witnesses should also be prepared to field any questions which the board members throw out. In selecting witnesses, you should choose only those people able to accurately represent your position, and who will be familiar with your circumstances. Make sure your witnesses know they have only a few minutes to speak.

If any (or all) of your witnesses are not going to be admitted, you should **tell** the board that you are going to read the statement(s) prepared by the witness(es). You should not ask them, you should **tell** them. Then, before they can say yes, no, or maybe, you should start reading. When you are done reading, or when the local board cuts you off, you should hand each board member a copy of the summary. The original should be handed to the chairperson of the board with a request that it be included in your file. By law, it **must** be.[21]

You now have the attention of each board member. The paper you have just given them is probably the only piece of evidence they have touched all day. Suddenly, the board members are interested. They have been made to feel important, because now they have something to do besides picking their noses or staring at the ceiling. They have a piece of paper to play with, and maybe even read.

Next, you should start in on your own statement. The procedure is the same here as for the witnesses. Keep in mind that timing is very important. DO NOT hand the board members their copies until you have read or paraphrased your statement. That way, you will probably get to make your points clear to the board. If the copies were handed in before giving testimony, you might be told that the board members will read them later. That could be a mistake, not only because the board might not read the statements at all, but also because it would destroy the impact necessary for getting the individual board members involved and interested. Get the picture? Make your point first, then turn them on to something they can read and ask questions about.

Another important technique is to try to have the testimony of witnesses given before yours. Should the fifteen minute time limit run out after you have testified, but before your witnesses have finished, the board can cut off further discussion by demanding that the witnesses either hand in their written statements or not, as they please. But if the fifteen minutes run out before you have had an opportunity to testify, it would probably be illegal for the board to terminate the hearing without allowing you to testify.

If you get interrupted in the middle of a point, or if for any reason you feel that you haven't gotten your point across (board members are not always swift on the uptake) you should use your notes to remind you of the points you need to make. You should not be afraid to make the same point more than once. Sometimes it is the only way to get through.

The board members may bombard you with questions. If so, you should try your best to answer them clearly and in as **few** words as possible. It is best to keep answers short and to the point, since the questions may come down in a rapid-fire attempt to confuse you. If given time, you should go ahead and expand your answer, but you should try to make your point in the first few words. That way, even if the answer is cut short, you have already said what you need to say.

When answering questions from the board members, it is good to keep in mind exactly what you are there to talk about. Don't let the board side-track you. If you are there to talk about your opposition to all war in any form, the differences between Buddhism and Catholicism don't make a damn bit of sense as a topic for discussion.

Above all else, you should keep cool. No matter what happens, do not lose your temper. If necessary, stop and take a deep breath. Call them all a bunch of bastards, but **silently.** For your own sake, you should **not** tell board members where to go. Sure, it would feel really great to tell them where they can put your file, how far up, and how long to leave it there, but it is only going to tear your case to shreds. If any board member treats you unfairly, seems biased, shows prejudice, or somehow shows that he or she is not familiar with the contents of your file, you should make a note to yourself about it. Get the board member's name, if possible, because it may come in handy later.

Another tactic the board may use is to sit there looking very uninterested and ask you what you want, or hit you with a statement like, "You are the third guy we have seen today who claims to be a conscientious objector. We turned down the others. What makes you different?" If that happens, you should take over the meeting. You should read your statement, have your witnesses present their testimony, tell the board everything you can think of that relates to why you should have your classification changed, and encourage the board members to ask questions. If they give you the ball, run with it!

Some time during the personal appearance you should make a specific point of explaining to the board why you feel that the board's reasons for initially denying your claim are not valid. It would probably be best to try not to offend board members in the process. In other words, you should be tactful. You will win much more support with a phrase like "Perhaps the board overlooked the fact that . . ." instead of coming out with something like, "Boy did you guys screw up."

At the end of the interview you should ask the board members if anything is unclear, or if there is any reason why they feel you do not qualify for the classification you are requesting. If one or more of your witnesses were not allowed to testify, you might ask the board if it will consider hearing from that witness now. When all is said and done, you should thank the board members for their time and leave the room.

On the way out, glance at a clock or watch and jot down the time, but do not leave the building yet. You should wait until the next person is called into the hearing room, and again record the time.

More paperwork

Next, walk out into the lobby and have a seat. This is where the real work starts. You should immediately write down as much as you can remember about what went on during the hearing. It doesn't have to be in order or exact wording, but you should get down everything you can recall. To begin with, stick to what actually went on, since that is what you will forget first. Note your comments and reactions later. If you feel that you were mistreated, make a note of how and by whom. If there were any questions you were not allowed to answer fully, note it and write out a full answer. Don't pretend that you answered completely at the appearance. Rather, you should play up the fact that the board did not allow you to answer fully. A typical entry might read, "Mr. Jones asked what I would do if someone raped my mother. I answered that I could not say, since the situation had never come up. I was about to add that under no circumstances would I kill the man when I was interrupted by Mr. Smith."

If there was any inference that board members were not familiar with your file, you should be sure to include that in your summary. For instance, "Mr. Smith asked if I were aware that I could have filed as a conscientious objector at an earlier time. I had to point out to him that I had done so. It seems that Mr. Smith was not at all familiar with my file."

If you feel that any or all of the board members treated you poorly, or didn't pay attention, discriminated against you in any way, or just generally bad-mouthed you, you should note it in your summary. If you feel that any of the questions asked were unfair or irrelevant, you should note it and explain why.

The reason for writing up a summary of the board meeting is that no actual transcript of the hearing is made. Unless you put together your own summation of what occurred at the board meeting, the only record will be whatever the board members or the executive clerk jots down and writes up for inclusion in your file, which in the past has usually meant little or nothing.

You may be wondering why you were instructed to jot down the time of day on three separate occasions. Believe it or not, there is a method to this madness. If you know what time you went in to the hearing, and what time the meeting ended, and what time the next man was called in, you can compute two very important bits of information. You will know how long the meeting lasted, which could be important if you feel you were not allowed enough time or if you were given less than fifteen minutes. The SS regulations provide that a man **must** be provided adequate time to fairly present his claim, and go on to say that "normally fifteen minutes will be deemed adequate" but if it appears that a man needs more time "the board shall extend the time."[22] Being told to leave after less than fifteen minutes denies a man the right to adequate time. Even if you were given twenty minutes, if you feel that it was not enough time to adequately present your claim, you should make that point in your summary.

You will also be able to compute the time from the moment you walked out of the hearing room until the next man was called in. Since the board votes immediately after hearing each case, you will know how much time the board spent discussing and voting on your claim. That information should also go into your summary.

While you are busily writing up your summary of the hearing, there are a couple of things your witnesses can be doing. If they were allowed in to testify, they should compose their own separate summaries of the meeting. If everyone was called in together they may want to help each other recall the details of the meeting and write up one group statement that everyone signs.

If for some reason any witness was not admitted to testify, that witness should write a letter to the local board expressing disappointment at not being allowed to testify. The letter might stress what an inconvenience it was to take all that time and trouble, just to be turned away. It might also say that unless the board felt it already had enough evidence to grant the requested re-classification, it was very arbitrary of them not to consider all of the available evidence in support of the claim.

When you have finished writing up your notes, take them home with you. Go over them later and see if you have anything to add. You may want to put things in chronological order. Put a statement at the end saying something like, "Unless I am notified otherwise, I will assume that the local board accepts my summary of the hearing as complete and accurate." Type up a clean final version and make copies of it for your file. Also gather up photocopies of the summaries written by your witnesses and save them in your file. All summaries should be mailed to the board by certified mail, return receipt requested.

Your summary and those of your witnesses should be dated, and should have your name and SS number on each page. The summaries should be mailed to the local board within a week of the personal appearance date. If you wait any longer than a week to submit a summary it may not carry as much weight.

Notification of results

Within a couple of weeks after the hearing you should hear from the local board. If you are granted the classification you requested, you probably won't want to mess with them any further. But, if you do want to mess with them, you have the right to question your new classification, which means another personal appearance and more stalling for time. However, you should use common sense. If you just got your 1-O conscientious objector status granted, and you request another personal appearance to go back and tell the local board members what a bunch of jerks they are, chances are good that you will get a brand new 1-A in the mail.

If you are turned down by the local board, there are many things to be done. You will have fifteen days in which to request a state appeal.[23] You have a right to a personal appearance before the state appeal board, just as in the case of a local board personal appearance.[24] However, you do not have the right to present witnesses at the appeal board level. As with the local board personal appearance, it is stongly recommended that you take advantage of all your rights. If you do not want a personal appearance with the state appeal board, you may still request that your file be sent to that board for review.[25]

Going about a local board personal appearance properly is a lot of work. As I keep saying, the SS just isn't very nice. If you want a classification other than 1-A you are going to have to work for it, but you can succeed if you are willing to put in the time and effort required.

All of the paperwork that you prepare and submit after your local board personal appearance can be used to your advantage at the state appeal. With a good case or a little bit of luck the state appeal board will reverse the decision of the local board and grant the classification you requested.

THE STATE APPEAL
AND BEYOND

This chapter is based upon the Selective Service Regulations as they existed during the Vietnam draft. It is possible that new rules will be issued for the next draft.

Shortly after your local board personal appearance you will be notified of the decision of the board. If your claim was granted, your notification will show that you have been given the classification you requested. If your claim was denied, you get the news.

If you are denied by the local board, all is not lost. You have fifteen days in which to request an appeal to the state appeal board.[1] At that time you may also request the right to appear in person before the state appeal board when it considers your file.[2] As with the local board personal appearance, it is suggested that you make full use of all your appeal rights. If you want a personal appearance with the state appeal board, but are living in a different state than the one you are registered in, you can request that your state appeal be transferred to the appeal board for the state you are now living in.[3] Unlike the local board "courtesy interview" discussed in Chapter 12, a transferred state appeal will be considered **and** decided finally by the board that hears your case. Even if you do not want a personal appearance with the appeal board, you still have the right to have the appeal board review your file.[4]

Checking the file

There are several things you should do before requesting a state appeal. The first is to tie up all the loose ends from your local board personal appearance. If you have not yet done so, you should make sure that your summary of the local board personal appearance, along with the statements of your witnesses and any other related paperwork, have been submitted to your file.

The next step is to find out why the local board denied your claim. The local board is required to give reasons for turning down a claim.[5] For a discussion of how to reply to the board's reasons, see Chapter 12. If reasons for denial were not sent along with the denial of your claim, it would probably be quickest and easiest for you to go down to your local board office and ask to see your file. If you are not able to do that yourself, you can request the board's reasons by mail, or you can authorize anyone else to review your file.[6] That procedure is outlined in Chapter 11. If possible, you should check your own file, since you know best what information you are looking for.

The board's reasons for denial may be on a separate piece of paper in the file, or if the local board wrote a summary of the personal appearance, the reasons for denial may be included as a part of the local board summary. Somewhere in the file there should also be a record of how the board members voted on your classification. That information may be useful, so you should get a copy of it. If possible, you should try to find out how each individual on the board voted. It is best for you to have photocopies of these documents, so you should ask the clerk at the local board to make copies on their machine. That service will cost twenty-five cents per page,[7] but there shouldn't be more than two or three pages.

While checking out your file you might as well make sure that your summary of the personal appearance and the statements of your witnesses are in the file. If they aren't, you should provide the board clerk with duplicate copies of them. You may also want to include copies of the mail receipts proving that you mailed the summaries to the board, along with a letter explaining that you are providing duplicate copies of the paperwork which the board seems to have lost. You might be rather upset about such carelessness on the part of your local board, and may wish to say so in your letter.

If for any reason the documents that were submitted at the personal appearance are not in your file, duplicate copies should immediately be submitted, along with a letter requesting a full explanation of where the originals have gone, and also asking whether the board members considered the documents when deciding to deny your claim.

If you go in to check your file and find that it is not in the local board office, you should immediately demand to see the head clerk and find out just what has been done with it. Chances are that if the file is not in the local board office at this point it has probably been sent to the state appeal board prematurely. That has been known to happen in cases where the local board is careless or trying to push a person through without giving him a fair chance. It is illegal for the board to send your file off unless you have requested a state appeal, or unless (very rare) an appeal has been ordered on the initiative of the State or National Director of the SS. Tell the head clerk that sending your file out is illegal, that you want it back and that the board is not allowed to send it out without your written request.

Anyone in this situation should also get off a letter or phone call to the State SS Director. Your draft counselor will have the address and phone number. In your communication with the State Director, you should explain that you have just found out about your file being prematurely sent to the state appeal board, and ask the

State Director for his personal attention to the matter. You should let the State Director know when your local board personal appearance was held, what the mailing date is on your latest classification notice, and that you have **not** requested a state appeal. You should explain further that you have more information to submit to your file before the state appeal, and ask that your file be returned to the local board office immediately, **before** being reviewed by the state appeal board. If the communication with the State Director is by telephone, you should send a letter (certified, return receipt, of course) confirming the phone conversation, including any promises made by the State Director.

If you really want to do a job of it, you can also request that you be sent written notice when the local board receives your file back, and that you be given a fifteen day period from the date of the written notice in which to prepare your file and request your appeal to the state board. You should be sure to indicate your name and SS number in all communications, and you might want to send your letter to the State Director by Special Delivery, as well as certified, return receipt.

In one case where a man had to send a letter to the State Director about his file being sent off prematurely, he received a very apologetic reply two days later, and all of his requests, including the request for an extension of time to appeal, were granted.

Preparing the file

Using the information gathered from the file, you should write up a statement explaining why you feel that the local board was wrong in not changing your classification. It may be that the board's reasons for denial were incorrect, that the reasons were not legal, that you feel the board failed to consider all of the available information, or any number of things. The point is: you know the board should have changed your classification, but it didn't, so it must have done something wrong. Your job is to make a good case for what that something was, and make it so clear that no one can fail to see it.

You may also want to have your draft counselor check your file to see if he or she can find any errors or illegalities. If so, you should be sure to point theme out to the appeal board in writing.

If you feel that you were treated improperly at the personal appearance, you should say so. If possible, you should point out exactly how, when, and by whom. You can use examples from your summary, the local board's summary, or anything else in the file to prove your points. If need be, you can also gather additional evidence to support your claim and add that to the file too.

You may be wondering if all this paperwork is really necessary. I feel that it is. Whether or not you have a personal appearance with the appeal board, you are going to want to have a file that is strong enough to support your claim in the face of a local board denial.

What is in the file? First, the evidence that you submitted before and during the personal appearance. Next, the local board's reasons for finding that information insufficient. If you leave it at that, you will lose the appeal. The state appeal board would simply uphold the local board's decision. So you submit your summary and the statements of your witnesses. Now you are even-up with the local board again. But you want to tip the scales in your favor, so you submit your statement explaining all the things you feel the local board did wrong. Now the appeal board will have only one of two choices. It can grant the classification you want, or it can come up with totally new reasons for denial.

There is a great deal of truth to the rumor that appeal boards tend to rubber-stamp the decisions of local boards. One big reason for this is that people in the past either didn't know how to prepare their file for a state appeal, or just didn't bother to do enough work. Those who have decided to live within the system, damnable as it may be, might as well know how to get what they want from it. The draft will not go away if ignored. The man who wants a deferment or exemption is going to have to want it badly enough to work for it.

The state appeal

Within the fifteen day deadline, you must write a letter to your local board requesting that your file be sent to the state appeal board. It is best if you have prepared your file by this time. If you want to appear personally before the appeal board, you must also request that in your letter. The request for a state appeal **must** be postmarked not later than the fifteenth day after the mailing date on your latest classificaton notice, and should of course be sent by certified mail, return receipt requested.[8] The request should include your name, the date, your signature, and your SS number. A copy should be kept for your personal file.

If you are requesting a personal appearance with the appeal board, you must be given at least fifteen days' notice of the date when the appeal board meeting will be held.[9] Your presentation at the appeal board meeting should be along the same lines as at the local board personal appearance, with the exception that you will not be allowed to present witnesses at the appeal board. You should be prepared to discuss your situation with the appeal board, and to point out to the appeal board members why you feel that the local board's decision was wrong.

After the state appeal board personal appearance you should prepare a summary of the meeting, just as you did after the local board meeting. Once again, you should take it home, clean it up, and submit it to your **local** board within a week of your meeting with the appeal board.

If you asked for a personal appearance before the appeal board, but for some reason you were unable to attend the meeting, you should immediately submit a written statement explaining why. If you submit your reason within five days, and if the appeal board feels that it is a good reason, it can decide to reschedule your appearance,[10] but it doesn't necessarily have to. If there is no time when you can expect to be able to meet with the appeal board, you should explain that to the board and request that it review your file.

After a state appeal you will be notified of the appeal board's decision by mail. Your next move will depend upon just what the notice says. If the appeal board grants the classification you want, that may be the end of it. However, you do have the right to question the new classification. If, for instance, you receive a 1-O classification from the appeal board, but also feel qualified for another classification, you can request a personal appearance with your local board within fifteen days of the mailing date of the 1-O classification notice.

If denied again

If your claim was denied by the appeal board, you should check the notice carefully. It should show the vote of the appeal board. If you are denied by a split vote (such as 2-1) at the appeal board, you have the right to appeal your classification to the national appeal board.[11] You will again have fifteen days in which to request the national appeal in the same way that you prepared it for the state appeal, making note of the reasons for denial given by both the local board and the state appeal board. If you are entitled to a national appeal, you also have the right to a personal appearance before the national appeal board.[12] Your letter requesting a national appeal can follow the same guidelines as your letter requesting the state appeal, and should be sent to your **local board.**

In most cases the vote of the state appeal board will be unanimous. If that is the case, you have no further right to appeal. If you are classified 1-A or 1-A-O and your lottery number has been reached, you can be ordered for induction immediately. A man in the same situation but classified 1-O can be processed for alternate service work. Some local boards in the past made it a practice to send people in this situation an induction order within a few days of the classification notice from the state appeal board, and some boards even sent the classification notice and an induction order in the same envelope. It saves postage.

Of course, if you are not in an eligible classification, or if it is not yet your year of eligibility, then you do have a bit of a breather left. Exactly what to do can best be worked out between you and your draft counselor.

There are several steps which can be taken even if the appeal board turns you down unanimously, although there is no guarantee that they will work. Anyone facing an induction order doesn't really have much to lose by trying them, and with a little luck you might get a national appeal granted.

Both the State SS Director and the National SS Director have the power to request a national appeal for a man, even if he was denied unanimously by the appeal board.[13] You may want to send a copy of your file to each of them and ask that they give the matter their personal attention. It would be a good idea for you to explain why you feel you were wronged by the state board.

The national appeal board itself can also choose to review cases, and it may be that a letter sent directly to that board would be helpful.

In cases of denied conscientious objector claims, the National Inter-Religious Service Board for Conscientious

Objectors (NISBCO), or the Central Committee for Conscientious Objectors (CCCO) may be able to persuade the national board to consider your file. Those organizations will need a copy of your file to work with, along with power of attorney to act on your behalf, so you should be sure to send those things. Their addresses are listed in Appendix B.

State Directors also have the power to make the state appeal board reconsider its decision.[14] You may want to write your State Director to ask him to do this in your case.

If you can come up with new evidence to submit in support of your claim, or if the reasons given by the state appeal board are not legal reasons for denial, it may be that you can get your case reopened.[15] Many conscientious objectors have found it helpful to write their local board a letter expressing their concern over the fact that their current 1-A status from the state appeal board means that they are going to be forced to refuse induction if ordered, since the SS didn't seem to understand that they are sincere in their beliefs. In the hope that the SS won't make them break the law, they ask their local board to reopen their classificaton. Don't do this unless you have thought it out very carefully and you **really** mean it!

Forced reopening is also a possibility, and can be very effective for people who need the time afforded by a double appeal process. Let's say that Jack Randolph is four months away from his twenty-sixth birthday, currently classified 1-A, and about to have his state appeal board hearing where he plans to pursue a 3-A hardship deferment. The day before his state appeal board appointment Jack turns in a conscientious objector claim to his local board. Since he has never before filed as a conscientious objector, and because the information he submits, if true, would warrant a change in his classification (from 1-A to 1-O), his local board must reopen his classification unless the state appeal board grants him a 3-A deferment.[16]

Let's say the hardship claim is denied by the state appeal board with a unanimous vote. About two weeks after his meeting with the state appeal board, Jack receives a 1-A classification **from his local board.** This is not the appeal board decision, but is notification that Jack's **local board** has considered his conscientious objector claim and denied it. He waits for the full fifteen days before he requests his local board personal appearance, and is not scheduled for another thirty days. His conscientious objector claim is denied by the local board, and two weeks later he receives a new 1-A from them. He again waits the full fifteen days before requesting his state appeal, and is not scheduled to meet with the state appeal board for another thirty days after that. By the time Jack's state appeal board appointment rolls around, the only thing that Jack has to tell them is that he had a helluva good time at his twenty-sixth birthday party the week before, and it really is too bad that they can't draft him anymore.

What course of action you should take after your state appeal is a matter that can best be decided by you and your draft counselor. There are a number of possible tactics, some discussed here and some not. The "best" thing to do will depend on two things - your classification, and what you hope to accomplish.

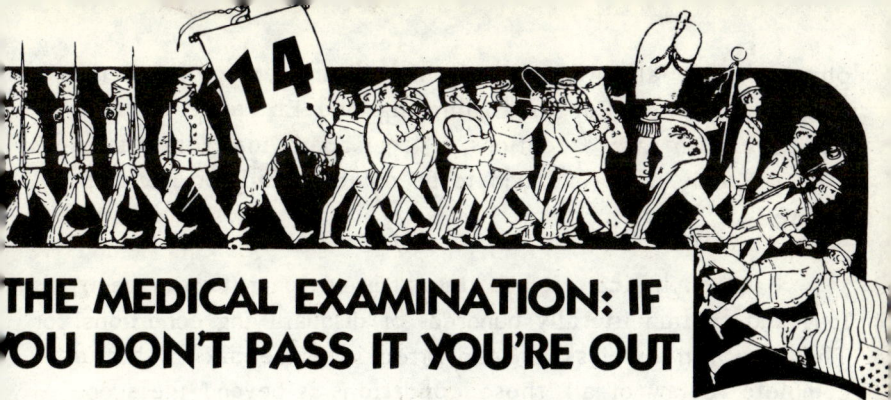

THE MEDICAL EXAMINATION: IF YOU DON'T PASS IT YOU'RE OUT

There are two kinds of classification for people who are considered to be physically, mentally, morally or administratively unfit for military consumption. The classification of 4-F is given to anyone who is permanently disqualified.[1] If someone is found temporarily disqualified, or has a condition which, if persistent, may be disqualifying, he is kept in his original classification (usually 1-A) but is placed into a special sub-class known as RBJ, and can not be drafted until he is given another physical examination and passes it.[2] RBJ means Re-examination Believed Justified.

It should be noted that once a person is classified 4-F he normally will not be re-examined. The 4-F classification is an exemption, meaning that anyone having a 4-F is exempt from the draft. The exceptions to the rule (aren't there **always** exceptions?) are cases where a person is found disqualified and is classified 4-F, but later becomes eligible under a changed or different set of medical standards, such as if he becomes a doctor, if war is declared, or if the physical fitness standards are substantially changed.[3]

The physical fitness standards

The physical fitness standards for induction are set out in Chapter Two of Army Regulation 40-501. The reason they appear in an Army Regulation rather than Selective Service Regulations is that draft physicals (and enlistment physicals for all branches of the military) are given at the Army-run Armed Forces Examining and Entrance Stations (AFEES). With rare exceptions, a local board may classify a man 4-F only if he is found to be not qualified for induction by AFEES.[4]

The physical fitness standards are over twenty pages long and contain literally hundreds of disqualifying conditions. The unabridged list is reprinted in Appendix C, but a complete review of all those conditions is beyond the scope of this book. It is important to note that many conditions which are disqualifying might seem almost trivial or even go unnoticed in civilian life. Do not just assume that you are physically fit, because roughly half of the people examined by AFEES over the years have been found not qualified.

The following review of the physical fitness standards does not begin to cover all of the disqualifying conditions listed. It is intended merely to get you thinking about possible eligibility for 4-F.

Abdominal Organs and Gastronintestinal System
Among the conditions listed are cirrhosis of the liver, hemorrhoids, recent hepatitus, current or recent hernias, intestinal obstructions, megacolon, pancreas diseases, herniated abdominal scars, and ulcers.

Blood System
Anemia, faulty RBC construction (including sicklecell anemia) Hodgkin's disease, and hemophilia, among others.

Ears and Hearing
Damage, disease or defect affecting inner or outer ear, perforation or severe scarring of the ear drum, hearing deficiency or loss.

Endrocrine and Metabolic

Diabetes, goiter, gout, hyperinsulinism, beriberi, pellagra and scurvy.

Extremities

Limitation of motion in shoulder, elbow, wrist, hand, fingers, hip, knee, ankle or toes; absence of all or most of a finger or toe; weak or "trick" knees, ankles, shoulders, elbows or wrists; claw toes, flat feet, hammer toes, severe ingrown toenails, arthritis, bone diseases, recurrent dislocated joint, badly healed or presently unhealed fractures.

Eyes and Vision

Numerous eye diseases or injuries are listed, such as chronic conjunctivitis, diplopia, glaucoma, night blindness, vision not correctable to 20/40 in one eye and 20/70 in the other, 20/30 in one eye and 20/100 in the other, or 20/20 in one eye and 20/400 in the other, refractive error greater than +8.00 or -8.00 diopters.

Genitorurinary

Absent or nondescended testicle, albuminuria, bedwetting, kidney diseases, amputated penis, prostrate gland hypertrophy.

Heart and Vascular

Organic valvular diseases, heart murmurs, dilated heart, high pulse rate, high or low blood pressure, varicose veins, rheumatic fever in past two years.

Height and Weight

Being too thin or too heavy can be disqualifying. For instance, at 5' 10" a person would have to weigh less than 123 or more than 214. Also, men less than 5' tall or more than 6' 8" are disqualified.

Lungs and Chest Wall

Abscessed lung, acute bronchitis, pleurisy, pnuemonia, recently fractured ribs, sternum, clavicle or scapula; active tuberculosis in past two years, bronchial asthma since age twelve, chronic bronchitis, pleurisy in past two years.

Mouth, Nose, etc.

Allergies, hay fever, asthma (chronic or severe), perforated septum, sinusitis.

Neurological

Degenerative disorders, frequent migraine, tremors, twitches, spasms, etc.

Psychological

Psychosis, neurosis, frequent encounters with police, antisocial attitudes, homosexuality, alcoholism, drug addiction, immaturity, learning defects.

Skin and Cells

Severe acne, dermatitis, eczema, chronic athlete's foot, chronic or severe sweaty palms or feet, extensive or deep scars, plantar warts, skin ulcers, obscene or extensive tattoos, psoriasis.

Spine

Bad backs are difficult to prove, but if verifiable by x-ray or medical history, may be disqualifying.

Miscellaneous

Moderate or severe reaction to bee stings or insect bites, acute deformities, chronic metallic poisoning, frostbite, chilblain, trench foot, predisposition to heatstroke or sunstroke, current or recurring venereal disease.

Documentation

In order to get a 4-F exemption you must have a condition that is considered to be disqualifying, and it usually must appear in the medical fitness standards. However, the AFEES can disqualify **anyone** who in their opinion would not make a good soldier, so any condition which could interfere with marching, jumping, running, standing, and other soldierly activities should be documented.[5]

Let's say you have chronic athlete's foot. (Yes, there are some good ones in the medical fitness standards!) The first big step in any medical claim is to document the condition - get it in writing. Now, whose opinion is the Army going to believe? A doctor, right? So you need to find a doctor who will help you to document your condition for the Army. You can start by asking your family doctor for help with the draft. It is always worth doing, since the worst the doctor can do is to say "no".

There is nothing illegal or unethical about documenting a medical condition. All you want your doctor to do is verify that you have something that is listed in the medical fitness standards. If you have one of the conditions listed you are legally entitled to be found not qualified for military service. It is your right, much like the right to vote or to assemble. And just like those rights, it will be denied to people who don't know the laws or don't insist on their rights.

It has been my experience that many doctors are pro-military, so you may be wasting your time (and money) with the family doctor, but you never know until you try. It is much better to work with your family doctor if he will cooperate, since he is the one you have been seeing for a number of years. But the really important thing is to have a **strong** doctor's letter, so if the family doctor will not make a commitment to be helpful, you should find another doctor.

In many areas of the country there are sympathetic doctors who will write dandy medical reports for draft registrants, provided the registrant has something worth writing about. Don't expect a "draft doctor" to lie, because he or she won't. But by the same token, a sympathetic doctor can write two pages about athlete's foot, whereas an unsympathetic doctor might write only two lines.

If you are having trouble finding a helpful doctor, you should contact a local draft counselor. If your doctor is sympathetic but not familiar with the medical fitness standards, show him or her Appendix C in the back of this book.

Fees will undoubtedly vary from one doctor to another, and fees will also depend on the services needed. While an office call for a blood pressure test may run just a few dollars, a complete draft physical examination can cost upwards of one hundred dollars or more. You should not ignore the possibility of a medical exemption just because you don't have a lot of money. Some doctors will accept monthly payments, and some will adjust their fees according to what you can afford to pay. But, please, please don't rip off a sympathetic doctor, or he may not be available to help the next guy who needs his services.

Once you have found a doctor who will be helpful, you should get the doctor to document your medical condition(s). If you have seen other doctors, you should get those records released to your current doctor. If not, you should explain to your doctor how long you have been aware of the condition and what problems you have had because of it. If you have a recurrent condition, such as athlete's foot, you should get in to see your doctor for treatment every time the condition crops up, and you should make sure that happens fairly often. With a condition such as athlete's foot, you should not just go to the local drug store and buy some foot powder to treat yourself. Sure, it is less expensive that way than going to the doctor, but what are you trying to save, your money or your freedom? A doctor's report is going to be much stronger if it can point to several bad attacks of athlete's foot over a period of months or years. That makes the condition "chronic", as required by the medical fitness standards. You should also remember that your doctor must have something current to document, so you should be sure to have a good case of athlete's foot on the day of your first appointment.

A number of people have regular physical examinations and have been told that they are in good health, so they conclude that they couldn't possibly fail their draft physical. Bear in mind that the purpose of a regular physical exam is to determine whether or not you have a condition that may cause you illness or injury in normal civilian life. A draft physical is given to determine whether or not you have a condition listed in the medical fitness standards.

Many people have conditions that would disqualify them from being drafted and don't even know about them, even though they have a physical exam each year. The fact that you are in good enough health to make the school football team has nothing at all to do with the fact that your athlete's foot is disqualifying. When in doubt, you should have a complete physical examination from a doctor who is familiar with the medical fitness standards.

The way the standards are written, roughly half the people examined at AFEES have been disqualified in the past. No doubt a higher percentage could have been disqualified, if only they had discovered and documented their condition in time.

Whether to see more than one doctor, and whether to see a doctor more than one time, depends upon your condition - both physical and financial. In many cases just one visit to a doctor is enough, as in cases of permanent disabilities. But consider this: the reason for any condition to be disqualifying is that the Army feels that the condition would interfere with your ability to function as a soldier - either that you would be on sick call all the time, or that the military environment would worsen the condition to the point where you would have to be discharged and possibly given disability payments.

In some cases, such as athlete's foot, a minor attack now and then won't really be a bother. The military can give you a little foot powder and that will be the end of it. On the other hand, if your doctor's report shows that in spite of all the foot powder and ointment prescribed you still can't seem to be without the rot for very long, that is another matter. After all, at home you can change your shoes and socks frequently, wash your feet once or twice a day, and so on. But the military can't guarantee that you will be able to do all of that at all times (especially if they have you marching around the deserts in the Middle East) so your condition is probably going to get even worse.

What to do with the report

You should have your doctor release the medical report letter to you. It should not be sent directly to the SS or the AFEES, for two reasons. First, you are going to want to read over the report, and go over it with your draft counselor to make sure that it is a strong letter. There is no advantage at all to submitting a wishy-washy doctor's letter. In fact, it could be a real detriment to your claim to have a letter in the file which down-plays a condition. Second, you are going to want to run off at least two or three more copies of your doctor's letter - one for your personal file, and at least the original and one copy to take with you to the AFEES physical exam. Remember: get the letter released to you, go over it with your counselor, and make several copies before going any further.

If the doctor's report is written shortly before you take your physical examination, it should suffice. But if the letter was written months previously, you should attempt to get a more recent letter from your doctor covering office visits or developments since the last letter was written.

The physical exam

Under the proposed mobilization plan (see Chapter 1), the pre-induction physical examination will be given on the day you report for induction. As such, it will be a last-ditch affair. If you fail the exam you will be sent home with an RBJ or a 4-F. If you are found acceptable you will be inducted into the military that day and sent off to a basic training camp. Because of this, it is extremely important that you show up for the physical exam with every piece of medical documentaton you can gather, and that you do your very best to be found unacceptable. There will be no second chance.

Let's take a look at a hypothetical pre-induction physical examination. The actual order in which things happen may vary from one AFEES to the next, and may even vary from day to day at each AFEES, but what we are interested in here is not the exact order, but some general guidelines.

Let's say that Phil is ordered to report for induction. It upsets him so badly that he forgets to change his socks for a week, and his athlete's foot crops up again. Poor Phil! He gathers up his doctor's letters about his recurring athlete's foot, and reports to the local AFEES as ordered, at around 7:00 AM.

Immediately upon walking through the door, Phil is assaulted by a screaming maniac who hands him a pile of forms to fill out. At that hour in the morning, who needs this fool? But Phil had better wake up and take a good look at what he is filling out. It could make the difference between passing and failing the physical examination.

One of the forms he has just been handed is the "Report of Medical History." Filling out this form properly can be to his advantage. He should particularly watch for question number eight, asking him to describe his present health. He may be **instructed** to fill in the words "I am in excellent health." But he is not in excellent health. To the contrary, he has a bad case of athlete's foot going for him that day, so he should ignore the instructions. A person may feel good, but still be in poor health. Phil should use the "Report of Medical History" form to explain that he has a case of athlete's foot, that it hurts, that he can barely walk because of it, and so on. The form also asks for a description of past medical history, so once again Phil should tell them all about it. He should make full use of the form. After all, they asked! And he should not forget to mention that he has letters from his doctor with him.

After being allowed "sufficient time" to fill out the forms, which may be quite a while, Phil and his friends will be herded into another room to take the mental test, a form of IQ exam. He shouldn't worry about failing it, since that is nearly impossible to do. If he found the AFEES that morning, he has a good shot at being found mentally capable of being a soldier. Of course, he could fail the test on purpose, but they have him covered on that angle too. There is an Army regulation which states that if anyone fails the mental exam, his school transcripts will be reviewed in order to determine his mental acceptability. If a man got through the eighth grade, he is likely to meet the mental standards. If he graduated from high school, he will automatically be found mentally acceptable.[6] I guess the Army figures that people like that are smart enough to figure out the wrong answers. Awfully considerate of them, isn't it?

After the mental test, which takes forever, the Army personnel will yell at Phil and his friends some more, and then herd them into another room to prepare for the actual physical examination. They will give each man a locker or basket for his clothing, and a cute little green bag to carry his valuables around in. The green bag is as good a place as any for doctors' letters. After all, they are very valuable.

Phil will be instructed to get undressed, except for his shorts, and to put his clothes into the basket or locker. It has been the experience of some people that the Army is embarrassed by nude bodies, and that anyone who forgets to wear shorts to his physical examination is told to go back and put his pants on, rather than run around nude. This creates quite a scene, so don't forget to wear shorts to your AFEES physical.

At the beginning of the physical, Phil may be instructed to hand in any doctor's letters which he has. If so, he should hand in one set, and keep the other set in his hot little hand (or his hot little green bag.)

Next, he will be herded through one station after another where examiners will weigh and measure him, give him an eye test (they count them - people with one to three eyes pass the test), a chest x-ray, instruct him to leak into a bottle (this is not a co-ordination test), take a blood sample, and check his blood pressure. At any of the stations where Phil thinks that he should fail, he should not take any guff from the examiner. He should explain to the examiner why he feels he should be disqualified, and not let up until he is disqualified. If the examiner refuses to disqualify him, Phil should jot down the station number and the examiner's name and move on.

Eventually our friend Phil will come to a point where there are several doctors sitting behind desks

interviewing people. It is usually best to pick the slowest line, since the faster a line moves, the less time that doctor is spending on each person. If Phil has not yet handed in his doctor's letters, or if he has handed them in but for some reason they aren't in his file (they do sometimes get "lost"), he should hand a set to the doctor now. He should be sure that the doctor reads his letters and considers them carefully. He should make the doctor examine him, and insist that he be disqualified. If someone at one of the previous stations refused to disqualify him, he should point that out to the doctor, and point out why that examiner was wrong. Phil should be especially sure to show the doctor his toes and tell him all about the problems of recurrent athlete's foot, and how he just can't seem to get rid of the disease. In short, he should do everything in his power to be found unacceptable.

Before leaving the doctor, Phil should ask him if he will be disqualified. If the doctor says that he is finding Phil acceptable, Phil should ask him why. He might explain to the doctor that chronic athlete's foot is disqualifying under Chapter Two, Section XVII, of Army Regulation 40-501, subsection 2-35(h), and that unless the doctor finds Phil unacceptable he is breaking the law and violating his rights.

If the doctor is still unconvinced, Phil should ask to see the officer in charge of the AFEES. In one successful case, a fellow jotted down the doctor's name and station number, and informed the doctor that he had a disqualifying condition, that he had a doctor's letter verifying that condition, and that unless he was found unacceptable, he planned to sue the doctor for malpractice. He was immediately sent to the officer in charge, who found him unacceptable. Doctors are more and more terrified by the words "sue" and "malpractice," especially when used in the same sentence. If all else fails, one can go all the way to the top and demand to see the commanding officer of the AFEES. If even he is no help, get his name as it may be needed later.

When Phil is finished with the interviewing doctor, he may be required to go through the rest of the physical examination even if he has been found unacceptable. If Phil has a letter from a psychiatrist (such as if he is gay or has emotional problems which should disqualify him) he will be given a short interview with a psychiatrist. Once again, he may encounter difficulty in being found unacceptable for induction, and should not allow himself to be brushed off or pushed around.

About the only fun things left are the mobility and flexion tests. Everyone will be told to take off his shorts and stand in a circle. The examiners will have people do push-ups, jump up and down, do deep knee bends, and so on. If a man is claiming a bad knee, shoulder, back or such, he **must** avoid doing anything which might strain his weak or bad body part. The examiners will undoubtedly holler at anyone refusing to follow instructions, but if a man goes ahead and successfully performs a motion which causes him pain or strain, he will likely be found acceptable regardless of his doctor's letters.

For example, I know a man who has a shoulder that dislocates almost any time he puts more than normal strain on it. At his physical examination the examining doctor read his letters, then instructed the man to do one push-up. He did it, and the doctor looked at him, looked at his doctor's letter, and found the guy acceptable. After all, his shoulder hadn't dislocated.

At the final check-out station you should be told whether or not you have passed the physical exam. If you have been found acceptable for induction, you will then be herded into yet another room (after being allowed to dress) where you will be inducted into the military. Immediately after the induction ceremony you will be an official member of the military, and will be ordered to get on a bus headed for a basic training camp. If you refuse that order, you will be subject to a military court-martial trial.

If you have been found unacceptable, either temporarily or permanently, you will be informed of it. Be sure to find out whether your disqualification is temporary or permanent. You will then be allowed to go home. If you have been found permanently disqualified you should shortly thereafter be re-classified 4-F by your local board.

Re-examination

If you are found unacceptable, this doesn't automatically mean that you will be classified 4-F. A large number of the conditions listed in the medical standards, such as high blood pressure, underweight and overweight, hemorhoids, broken bones, and so on, are considered to be temporarily disqualifying conditions. It is therefore completely possible for you to fail your physical examination but not be re-classified 4-F because the Army feels that re-examination at a later date is justified. If that occurs you will keep your classification (1-A, 1-A-O or 1-O) but will be placed in the special "hold" category, RBJ. People in the RBJ category cannot be drafted until they pass a re-examination.[7]

At some later date, perhaps a few weeks, perhaps as long as a year, you will be called back to AFEES for a physical re-examination. If you fail the second examination for the **same** reason that you failed the first examination you should be found permanently disqualified and re-classified 4-F. But if you fail the re-examination for a **new** reason (such as if you were disqualified at the first physical because of a broken arm, then fail the second physical for another temporary condition, such as blood pressure) you can be re-called for further examination. If you fail the second physical examination for a permanent reason, such as being gay, you will not be re-examined. Lastly, should you be found acceptable at the second examination, you may be inducted into the military that day.

Being gay

Up until the late sixties a person would almost automatically receive a 4-F exemption by simply claiming homosexuality. Word quickly got around, with the result that thousands of men started claiming to be gay at their AFEES examination, regardless of their true sexuality. It wasn't long before the psychiatrists at AFEES refused to believe anyone claiming to be gay, including gay men. In fact, in at least one case the psychiatrist refused to disqualify a truly gay man because, "he didn't look like one". The AFEES refused to find him unacceptable, so the man refused induction. At trial he was convicted of refusing induction despite ample proof of his homosexuality.[8]

At this time it appears that being gay is still a valid basis for obtaining a 4-F exemption.[9] But as with any 4-F exemption, you will have to prove your homosexuality by use of medical evidence. Since homosexuality has been removed from the American Psychiatric Association's list of character and behavior disorders, some psychiatrists may refuse to document a man's homosexuality as a psychiatric phenomenon. But some psychiatrists are still willing to provide such documentation, and of course should be consulted by a gay man seeking to avoid the draft.

If a gay man has ever seen a psychiatrist or a medical doctor for any gay-related problems, he should get a report from that doctor. For instance, men who have seen a psychiatrist for help with sexual identity problems or emotional difficulties stemming from being gay should be able to prove their sexuality in that way. It is also worth remembering that the doctor who performs a gay man's periodic verereal disease testing is likely to be aware that he is gay, and should be able to write a report stating that the kinds of testing the man has requested (especially throat and/or anal cultures) are necessary only for gay men. Any other means of proving homosexuality in a medical report should also be explored. If possible, a man's report should also show why his being gay will interfere with his ability to act as a soldier, since that is the ultimate question.

For men who are not gay, claiming homosexuality is **not** an "easy way out" of the draft. To the contrary, providing false information is a violation of the draft law punishable by up to five years in prison and/or a $10,000 fine.[10] Merely claiming to be gay, or showing up at AFEES wearing women's clothing, is not likely to work, and will only make it more difficult for gay people to be exempted.

Some unusual cases

Some people have found that they have no disqualifying conditions, but have devised ways of appearing to have conditions which would make them unacceptable. The following examples are given only to show how the pressures of the draft can cause you to be dishonest. I certainly don't encourage anyone to do any of these things, as they are highly illegal, and some are downright unhealthy.

One young man had his room-mate, a medical student, put a plaster cast on his arm the evening before his scheduled induction. Naturally the people at AFEES took it on good faith that the fellow had a broken arm, and they sent him home with a temporary disqualification. Such a practice is called conspiracy to evade the draft, and could get you into a lot of trouble if you were to get caught at it.[11]

Some people have impregnated a cigarette with India Ink, then smoked it. Apparently the ink stains the smoker's lungs and appears in an x-ray to be tuberculosis. This could be very dangerous to one's health.

There have been stories about people putting "additives" in their urine samples. One fellow found out that albumin in the urine is disqualifying, so he stuck some dried egg (very high in albumin) under his fingernails, then deposited it in his urine sample. Unfortunately for him the examiners immediately realized that if he really had that much albumin in his urine, he would be very ill, if not dead. He was prosecuted for providing false information in an attempt to gain an exemption from the draft. Another person tried the same thing, but put in so little albumin that it went unnoticed at the physical examination.

A very popular thing to do at one time was to conceal a pin in the lining of one's shorts, prick a finger with it, and squeeze a few drops of blood into the urine. It was thought that this would appear to be kidney infection. However, kidney infections are characterized by the presence of dead blood cells in the urine, not live ones. Furthermore, very few people realized that if one truly has a kidney infection the bladder is usually quite sensitive, and failed to respond properly when prodded by the doctors.

Another very popular "trick" has been to use drugs, especially amphetamines, to give a person high blood pressure. Since most AFEES doctors are aware of such tactics, it is usually difficult to fool them. The old stand-bys of using coffee or caffeine tablets, not sleeping for a day or two, or smoking lots of cigarettes, have been used quite a bit, but are usually ineffective unless a person's blood pressure normally runs a bit high. In cases of blood pressure, the AFEES will often insist on morning and afternoon blood pressure tests for three consecutive days, so any artificial stimulation of one's blood pressure would have to be effective for a prolonged period of time.

People have been known to strap coins tightly to their arms or legs for several days before a physical exam, causing what appear to be external ulcers. Some people have applied chemical irritants to their skin, or in some other way caused themselves to come down with a case of skin rash or dermatitis.

There is also a story about a fellow who pretended to be hard of hearing. He was tested several times, and each time responded only to the loudest sounds. When the examiners were done testing him they pointed him toward an open door and indicated that he could leave. As he walked out he was softly instructed to close the door behind him. Without thinking, he reached for the door knob, and passed his hearing test.

A common occurence many musicians have noticed is that after playing for a while, especially in a loud electric band, one can't hear properly for several hours. There have been people who spent the night before their physical examination playing music or listening to their stereo loudly through a set of headphones. They turned the volume up as loud as they could stand it and played hour after hour of loud music, numbing their ears. As a result, they couldn't hear properly for hours. Many failed the hearing test at the AFEES. However, it should be noted that there is scientific proof that loud music can cause a permanent hearing loss. In one experiment, several rats were totally deafened for life after exposure to persistent loud music. So, don't let your pet rat turn up the volume too much - it could make him go deaf.

One last example is sickening to relate. One man drank no liquids for twenty-four hours before his induction physical exam. Then, just before leaving the house in the morning he drank down an entire quart of vinegar. When it came time for the AFEES to test his urine it was almost pure acid, and they were unable to test it. The examiners knew that he had done something, but they couldn't figure out just what it was that he had done, so they sent him home with a temporary disqualification. I would imagine that he was probably sick for a day or two afterwards. He was a sick civilian, but he soon had to face another examination.

Of course we have all heard stories about people shooting off toes or fingers, getting obscene tattoos, or otherwise mutilating their bodies to stay out of the draft. That sort of thing will usually work, but if anyone is so desperate to avoid the draft that he would seriously consider a life-long mutilation of his body, he should first exhaust every other possible avenue. I suggest going to a sympathetic psychiatrist and documenting the emotional problems he is experiencing.

It is true that psychiatrists are not inexpensive. A good psychiatrist may cost several hundred dollars by the time a man is through. But, after all, how much money is a toe or finger worth? More than that, how much money is peace of mind worth?

Generally a person is better off to consult a psychiatrist rather than a psychologist, or an orthopedist rather than a chiropractor, since the AFEES gives more weight to letters from medical doctors.

Conclusion

All things considered, there is no reason for anyone to be drafted who doesn't want to be drafted. Under current medical fitness standards, it is fact that roughly fifty percent of the people examined by AFEES have been found unacceptable for induction. With knowledge of the medical fitness standards and proper medical documentation, no doubt even more people would qualify for the 4-F exemption.

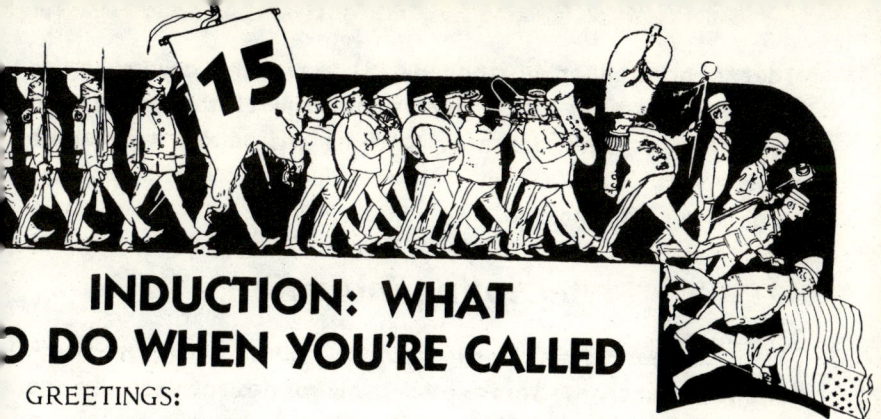

INDUCTION: WHAT
O DO WHEN YOU'RE CALLED

GREETINGS:

YOU ARE HEREBY ORDERED FOR INDUCTION INTO THE ARMED FORCES OF THE UNITED STATES . . .

Hundreds of thousands of men have opened letters from the SS to read those words. Most people who have been ordered for induction will never forget the day it happened. For some it comes as a shock, since they have been trying to convince themselves that it somehow wouldn't happen to them. Even a person who feels prepared may still find it difficult to realize that his life is being completely disrupted and changed.

For far too many men, it is only the receipt of an induction order that causes them to finally start thinking about how they feel about going into the military. Many see the induction order as an inescapable doom. While it is true that men who start thinking about the draft earlier have a better chance, receipt of an induction order is not the end of the line. Under the proposed mobilization plans (Chapter 1) men who receive an induction order will still have a chance to gain deferment or exemption, provided that they act **very** quickly. I do not encourage men to wait until the last minute, but those who do should not feel that they are beyond hope.

There are basically four possible courses of action that a person with an induction order can take. You can (1) accept induction into the military, (2) get your induction order cancelled or postponed, (3) leave the country or go underground, or (4) refuse induction. Some of the choices are legal, while others are not. Nothing will make the whole mess go away, so a man with an induction order is going to need to decide quickly.

Accepting induction

The first and most obvious course of action is to accept induction. Some people who decide to accept induction have been able to adjust to the military environment with a minimum of problems. Others have found that the military is not for them, and many have been successful in obtaining various types of discharges after only a few weeks or months in the military. There are some points that should be considered by anyone who is thinking of accepting induction in order to try for a discharge. First, most reasons for discharge from the military are also reasons for deferment or exemption by the SS. It might make more sense for you to pursue classification through the SS rather than to go into the military in order to get out of the military. Another point is that going for a military discharge may be more difficult than being deferred or exempted by the SS, and may involve quite a bit more discomfort and emotional strain, as well as a lot of legal problems.

Since military law is very different from civilian law or Selective Service law, and since the military usually makes it difficult or impossible for inductees to get reliable counseling, it would be a good idea for anyone considering this alternative to do quite a bit of talking with a counselor or lawyer schooled in military law.

For some people, accepting induction may be the safest alternative. For instance, if your time limit for requesting deferment or exemption has already run out, you may be facing the choice of refusing induction followed by possible prosecution, or accepting induction. Likewise, a review of your file may show a valid defense to a charge of refusing induction (such as wrongful denial of a claim for conscientious objector status) but also show a strong possibility that you could be convicted of some other draft law violation, such as failure to provide a current address, to which you have no defense. In such situations many men prefer the choice of accepting induction for the purpose of seeking a military discharge, rather than to face an almost certain conviction should they refuse induction.

Even men with a seemingly good defense to a charge of refusing induction and no other possible charges, may choose to accept induction rather than face the possibility of being convicted in the courts and sent to prison. It is really a question of where you want to end up if you lose. If you refuse induction and lose, you may end up in prison. If you accept induction to seek discharge and lose, you will end up in the military. It is not an easy choice.

Requesting immediate discharge

The following procedures are suggested for anyone who decides to enter the military in order to try for a discharge. The sooner after entering the military that discharge is requested, the better the chances of having the request granted. It may be that the person who requests discharge the same day he is inducted will not get proper attention, in the belief that a few weeks in the military will "straighten him out". However, that procedure is probably illegal, and action can be taken if it occurs. The person who waits several weeks or months before applying for discharge runs the risk of having the military feel that he has already shown that he can function in the military (unless he has been AWOL or in some other way proved his unacceptability, which is not recommended since it could result in a military prison sentence).

Many people have had a great degree of success in applying for discharge the same day they were inducted. In most cases these people have been discharged within two or three months, and in some cases more quickly. The first point for a man in this situation to consider is his reason for requesting discharge. Unfortunately, the military does not hand out discharges to anyone who requests one. You must have a legal reason for your request, such as conscientious objection, erroneous induction, or so on.

To qualify for discharge as a conscientious objector you must show that your objection "crystallized" or changed substantially since your induction. There is also a provision for draftees who can show that a conscientious objector claim filed with the SS was improperly processed. In most cases where a conscientious objector claim was previously filed with the SS, it is better if you can show that your objection has become even stronger since your induction order was sent to you. People who file a request for discharge as a conscientious objector which is basically the same claim as the one the SS denied will not get a discharge.

Anyone who files for discharge as a conscientious objector **must** be placed on duty which provides the "minimum practicable conflict" with his beliefs.[1] This means that once you have filed, you cannot legally be ordered to handle or train with weapons, or in any way violate your CO beliefs. Generally, the inductee who files for a conscientious objector discharge immediately after entering the military will be held at the Reception Station at the basic training base while his discharge application is processed. The "minimum conflict" clause remains effective until the conscientious objector claim has been finally approved or disapproved by the Pentagon.

To qualify for an erroneous induction discharge you must be able to show that you should not have been inducted in the first place, such as if you were wrongfully denied a deferment or exemption, if you should not have been found qualified under the medical fitness standards, and so on.

As an example of erroneous induction, let's go back to the situation we discussed in the chapter on medical exemptions - a man not qualified because of chronic athlete's foot.

On induction day, Dexter Ryan showed up with a rampant case of athlete's foot and three doctors' letters: one from two years previously, one from two months previously, and one dated four days before his induction date. He tried his best to fail the physical examination, but for some reason was found acceptable, and decided to accept induction. He does not meet the physical fitness standards, should not have been inducted, and therefore qualifies for an erroneous induction discharge.

Sometimes it works well to apply for discharge for several different reasons. For instance, let's say that in addition to his athlete's foot, entry into the military has also made Dexter realize that he is a conscientious objector. He can apply for an erroneous induction discharge because of his athlete's foot **and** for a conscientious objector discharge, both at the same time.

As soon as possible after induction Dexter should start looking for someone to present his discharge requests to. By the time he finally gets them into the right hands, half of the people on base are going to know that he is a "trouble maker" and the sooner they get rid of him the better it will be for the military.

Further, since Dexter is requesting discharge as a conscientious objector, the military is likely to feel that he may start "infecting" other recruits with his ideas. In no time at all he might have every recruit on the base filing for a conscientious objector discharge, and because of the "minimum conflict" rule, that would mean they could not conduct basic training, since none of them could be ordered to train with weapons. Not only is Dexter a trouble maker, he is a potential subversive as well! Hopefully, the military is going to realize they have nothing to gain and much to lose by keeping Dexter around, and will find the quickest, easiest way possible to get rid of him. Usually that would mean granting the erroneous induction discharge, but no matter which discharge request is granted, it will give him a discharge under honorable conditions.

Often, of course, things don't go quite so smoothly as we might wish. It may be that both of Dexter's discharge requests are turned down. If so, he should be in touch with a civilian lawyer who handles military cases. In a great many cases he or she will be able to get Dexter discharged by filing a "habeas corpus petition" in federal court. In fact, Dexter may be wise to retain his attorney **before** entering the military. His lawyer can help prepare the discharge requests, and also help during the processing as well. If Dexter is filing for an erroneous induction discharge, his lawyer can file a habeas corpus petition on the day he accepts induction. That way, he can go directly to court witout having to be processed by the military, which could save weeks or months of time. If he doesn't want an attorney, or would rather wait to see if he needs one, he should certainly work closely with a counselor who is familiar with military law.

Postponement or cancellation

The second possibility for someone with an induction order is to get the order cancelled or postponed. Under the proposed mobilization plan, everyone will be presumed to be classified 1-A for purposes of ordering them for induction. However, a man receiving an induction order will be allowed a brief period of time in which to request deferment or exemption.[2] It would seem that making such a request within the time limit should entitle you to at least a postponement of your induction date.[3] The only exception seems to be a claim for 4-F exemption (Chapter 14). Since 4-F status is determined by AFEES rather than the local board,[4] and since the pre-induction physical examination will be given on the date set for induction,[5] men claiming a 4-F exemption will most likely be instructed to bring their doctor's letter to AFEES on their scheduled induction date. However, men who claim any other deferment or exemption should have their induction postponed or cancelled, although they may still be required to report for a physical exam on that date.

The law also provides that a full time high school or college student who receives an induction order may have his induction postponed until the end of the term.[6] High school students are entitled to a postponement until graduation from high school or age twenty, whichever occurs first. If you are a high school dropout, this is one more strong reason to go back for your diploma.

Any induction order which has not been legally issued must be cancelled. For instance, are you classified 1-A or 1-A-O? If not, you cannot be ordered for induction.[7] Have you requested appeal rights, or do you still have time left to do so?[8] Is the date to report for induction long enough after the mailing date of the induction order?[9] Is this your year of eligibility, and have you been placed in the correct Priority Group?[10] Have you presented a claim for deferment or exemption that forces the local board to reopen your classification and afford you new appeal rights?[11] You should never assume that your induction order is legal, but should have a counselor or lawyer check it for you. Many induction orders in the past have been found to be illegal. A man in that situation should immediately inform his local board of the illegality of the induction order and demand that the order be cancelled.

Even if an induction order is otherwise legal, the local board has the authority to cancel or postpone induction in cases of death, serious illness or extreme emergency in your family.[12] The State SS Director and the National SS

Director also have the power to postpone your induction for almost any reason.[13] If you feel that you have a good reason for requesting postponement or cancellation of your induction order you might wish to contact one or more of the above to explain in writing why your induction should be cancelled or postponed. At this point you have nothing to lose by trying. Your request should be sent by wire with a confirmation copy sent to yourself, or by Special Delivery mail, certified, return receipt requested.

In cases where you first become eligible for a deferment or exemption after receipt of an induction order, and your change of status is the result of circumstances beyond your control, the local board has the power to cancel your induction order, reopen your classification, and afford you new appeal rights.[14] However, the courts have held that becoming a conscientious objector after receipt of an induction order and after the time to claim such status has expired is not a circumstance beyond the registrant's control.[15] Men in this situation are required to accept induction and present their conscientious objector claims to the military for processing, unless some other means can be found to postpone or cancel the induction order.

Leaving the country

The third possibility, that of moving from the United States (or "going underground" within the US) is a very big decision. Doing so is, of course, illegal. And unlike the Vietnam times, it seems likely that people choosing this option will **not** be given any form of amnesty or clemency in the future.

One of the problems with such a choice is that there are very few places left to go. Canada and Sweden, both sympathetic to US draft evaders during the Vietnam war, have let it be known that they no longer welcome draft evaders. Many foreign countries have a draft of their own, and US draft evaders moving to those countries could find themselves facing the draft in another country. Should a draft evader ever be deported from his new country back to the United States, he would most likely find a "welcoming committee" waiting for him: the FBI. If he left the United States and renounced his US citizenship, he would then be either a stateless person or an alien (citizen of another country). Under the regulations of the Immigration and Naturalization Service, he could be barred from ever re-entering the United States, even as a visitor.

Going underground has similar problems. If caught, a prosecution and conviction would be very likely. Even if not caught, the rigor of being a fugitive, establishing a new identity, avoiding old friends and acquaintances, and so on, can result in a paranoid and unpleasant existence.

There are many legal options available for avoiding the draft. Anyone considering leaving the country or going underground should think through his decision very carefully before making a move which could affect the rest of his life.

Refusing induction

This section is not intended to encourage anyone to refuse induction. Even in cases where a person may seem to have a legally sound reason for refusal, complications can arise which result in being convicted of a felony.

For thousands of people, the best answer to their draft problem seems to be to refuse induction into the military. This is especially true for people whose conscience will allow them to cooperate with the system to the point of attempting to gain some legal means of avoiding induction, but who feel that they cannot accept induction into the military under any circumstances. There are basically two ways to refuse induction: failing to report for induction when ordered, or reporting but refusing to submit to induction into the military.

Some people come to feel that to comply with the draft system in any way would be wrong, so they do not show up on their induction date. Usually the SS will give you another chance by sending a second reporting date. If that date is ignored as well, the FBI will likely be coming around looking for you, if they didn't come looking the first time. Unless they have an arrest warrant, you do not have to let them into your home or answer any of their questions. Perhaps the best thing to tell the FBI agents is that you will have your lawyer contact them, and that you have nothing further to say at that time. Do not get tricked into talking to them as they are just trying to make a case against you.

There are problems with a "no show" refusal of induction, especially since the man who is given another reporting date and still does not report may stand a higher chance of conviction than the man who reports but refuses induction.

Perhaps the cleanest way to refuse induction is to show up at the proper time and place, go through the pre-induction processing, but **refuse** to be inducted into the military. This way, you might be found unacceptable during the pre-induction physical examination and be given a 4-F exemption (see Chapter 14).

It is possible to show up for induction at a station other than the one you are ordered to. In order to be processed, you may be required to show up at your chosen alternate location at least seventy-two hours before the time you were ordered to report.[16] This transfer of AFEES can be convenient for people who are living a great distance from the station they are ordered to, and it can also be useful to the person who is trying to be found physically unacceptable.

Let's say that Peter Lopez is ordered to report for induction at the Los Angeles AFEES on the twenty-eighth of the month. Peter has chronic athlete's foot, and plenty of doctor's letters to verify his condition. However, Peter's draft counselor informs him that the Los Angeles AFEES is one of the worst stations in the country for taking a physical examination. His draft counselor also informs him that reports from draft counselors in Massachusettes indicate that the AFEES in Springfield has been finding a lot of people unacceptable lately.

On the twenty-second of the month, Peter reports to Springfield AFEES for induction. Since he is reporting well in advance of his scheduled induction date, he will be processed. If he is found unacceptable for induction by the doctors at the Springfield AFEES, his induction order will be cancelled and he will not have to report to the Los Angeles AFEES. But if he is found **acceptable** for induction at Springfield, he must either accept induction there or, if he refuses induction in Springfield, he will still be under orders to report to the Los Angeles AFEES on the twenty-eighth. In other words, he **must** report for induction at the time and place ordered, **unless** he has been found unacceptable at some other AFEES prior to his reporting date. If Peter is found acceptable by the Springfield AFEES he will want to report to the Los Angeles AFEES for two reasons: it will give him another chance to be found unacceptable because of his athlete's foot, and it will allow him to formally refuse induction if he is not found physically disqualified.

When ordered to report for induction you will be given a complete pre-induction physical examination on the day you report to the AFEES. Many people - roughly fifty percent of those who report - are found unacceptable at this point and given either a temporary or permanent medical disqualification.

If you are planning to avoid induction for medical, psychological or moral reasons, induction day will be your one big chance to be disqualified. You may want to let the examining doctors know that you plan to refuse induction if found qualified, and why. You also may want to ask the doctors for their names, in case you decide to sue them for medical malpractice should they find you acceptable. Men in this situation are advised to re-read Chapter 14. It may make the difference between being sent home with a 4-F exemption or having to refuse induction.

If you plan to refuse induction on grounds of conscience (such as if your conscientious objector claim was denied by the SS, or if you don't believe in the draft) you may wish to talk about your feelings at the AFEES. You never can tell what will happen. One person whose conscientious objector claim had been turned down decided to refuse induction. At the AFEES he took the time to explain his beliefs to everyone he met, to let them know that he was only there for the purpose of formally refusing induction. About half way through the processing an officer took him aside, listened to his entire story, and then sent him home. Two weeks later he received a new classification card in the mail, with a 1-O classification on it. It isn't in the regulations, but it did work at least once.

Another person printed up a full page statement explaining that he felt the military was immoral, and proclaiming that he planned to refuse induction. His statement also encouraged others concerned about the immorality of war and imperialism to refuse induction along with him. He handed out his flyers in front of the AFEES and spent the entire morning discussing the situation with anyone who would listen to him. He was found unacceptable for induction and sent home with a 4-F exemption. Again, a long shot, and a possibility of prosecution for encouraging others to violate the law. But it did work at least once.

Much of the induction process involves filling out papers and standing in lines. The important moment comes when you are taken to a large room for the actual induction ceremony. Everyone will be lined up and told to step forward when their name is called. **Don't** take that step if you plan to refuse induction!

It is the act of stepping forward that constitutes induction. Contrary to popular belief, taking the oath of induction occurs **after** induction, and refusing to take the oath is punishable under military law, since a man is already in the military at that time.

If you plan to refuse induction, you should not step forward when your name is called. Just to make sure that there is no question about it, you should also say out loud that you refuse induction. There is no danger of anyone pushing you forward or anything like that; it is just that you want to make sure the officials understand what you are doing. Sometimes people in the Army aren't too bright.

If you refuse to take the step forward, an Army officer will probably take you quickly into a private room. After all, they don't want you infecting others with your weird ideas. You will likely be told the penalty for refusing induction is five years in jail and a ten thousand dollar fine, that it is a federal felony offense, and that you will be sent to prison if you refuse induction. The Army will do everything in their power to scare you. Then, they will probably offer you another chance to step forward. I am sure we can all appreciate their thoughtfulness.

If you resist their efforts to get you to step forward, they will probably ask you to make or sign a statement that you have willfully refused induction. I strongly recommend that you **refuse** to make such a statement. If you do give such a statement, it is an admission or confession which can be used against you in a court of law. It is never a good idea to admit that you are guilty of any crime, at least not until you have consulted a lawyer.

After refusing induction you may be arrested. People are usually just told to go home, and that they will be contacted later, but every once in a while a person is actually taken from the induction center to a police station for booking. If you are arrested on the spot, you will probably be let go on your own recognizance after booking, unless they have reason to think you may not show up, or unless they are in a bad mood. Being released without bail means they trust you to show up for trial. However, just in case the police do decide to hold you, you should arrange for bail ahead of time. It would be a good idea for you to write the phone number of your lawyer, friend or bail bondsman on your arm with a ballpoint pen before induction. That way, even if the police take away your clothing and your wallet (a common booking procedure) you will still have the phone number handy.

What happens after refusal

After induction processing has been completed, all files are returned to the SS.[17] The files of those who have refused induction will be forwarded to the United States Attorney's office, where a decision will be made whether or not the government wants to prosecute. The US Attorney will usually not bring charges unless he feels he can win the case. Even though the US Attorney screens cases pretty thoroughly, it is interesting to note that in the past people were rarely convicted of refusing induction, and even more rarely were any given prison sentences. During the early seventies, over ninety percent of the people who refused induction were not prosecuted.[18] Of the few who were taken to court, well over half were found not guilty. For example, in the fiscal year ended June 30, 1971, there were 2,973 Selective Service cases that got to court. While that was a higher number than in any year since 1945, it still represents less than ten percent of the people who refused induction. Of the people taken to court, only 34.8% were convicted, and of those convicted only 36% were sent to prison. So, only about 13% of the court cases resulted in a person being sent to prison.[19] Of course, the figures could be different next time around, and statistics don't help if you are the one guy in one hundred who ends up in the slam. Still, the figures are interesting. For more on this see Chapter 16.

There is another thing that you should consider if you are thinking of refusing induction. You can be taken to court on more than one charge. The US Attorney's policy during the later Vietnam era seemed to be moving toward a position of trying to convict people, regardless of the charge, if they refused induction. In other words, even if the government couldn't make the charge of "refusing induction" stick, they were just as happy to nab people on some other charge, such as late registration or failure to report an address change. There have even been cases of people being acquitted of refusing induction, and then being taken back into court on some other charge and convicted.

If the government decides not to prosecute, you may get a letter from either the US Attorney or your local board, instructing you to report at once to your local board office. Upon reporting you may be informed of the decision not to prosecute, or you may be told that a previously denied classification will be reconsidered by the board.

Another possibility is that you may simply be sent a new classification from your local board. Usually, if you are reclassified by the local board after refusing induction, you are well on the way to the classification you want. In many cases the board will simply send it to you, but sometimes you will be sent a new 1-A classifiction and will have to start your appeal process all over again. In rare cases even the second appeal may be shot down, and you may once again end up with an induction order. One person I know got seven induction orders before his local board finally gave in and granted him a 1-O classification.

If the US Attorney decides to prosecute, there may be a warrant issued for your arrest. You or your lawyer can check this out by calling the US Marshall's office and asking if there is a warrant out in your name. In some cities the Marshall is very civil about the entire affair. An officer will call on the phone to ask if you would like to come down and surrender. If you agree, they will usually book you and then release you on your own recognizance. But just in case the Marshall in your area isn't so considerate, you or your lawyer should check from time to time to see if a warrant has been issued. If so, you might call them and offer to surrender.

If you don't surrender, or are not given the opportunity to do so, the Marshalls will come looking for you. There is nothing more inconvenient than being rousted out of bed at three in the morning just to be arrested . . . or being arrested on a Friday night and not being able to raise bail or see a magistrate until Monday morning. It's much more tolerable to deal with the police at a civilized time of day, and on your own terms.

Another way to avoid unnecessary hassle over being arrested might be for you or your lawyer to send a letter (certified, return receipt, of course) to the Marshall's office explaining that you are willing to surrender to any warrant if the Marshall will just be good enough to give a call or send a letter and let you know when and where to surrender.

Looking for a lawyer

If you are going to refuse induction you will probably need a lawyer. You could choose to defend yourself, but in my experience, judges tend to be harsher on defendants who insist on representing themselves.

The first person to ask about a good draft lawyer is your draft counselor. The counselor may be a lawyer or may be able to refer you to a good one. In many areas of the country there are groups of lawyers who specialize in handling Selective Service cases. Those people are usually quite good in their area of law, and are sometimes able to take cases for relatively low fees if you are not able to pay the full fee. Lawyers' fees will vary. Some lawyers charge an hourly rate, while others charge a flat fee. Some charge very little, while others charge quite a lot. There is a saying that you get what you pay for. To some extent this is true with lawyers, although it might be more accurate to say that you pay for what you get. The more skillful draft lawyers usually have a good reputaion and can afford to charge higher fees for their services, but there are a lot of excellent lawyers who don't charge big fees. Even though an expensive lawyer may be a good lawyer, it doesn't necessarilly follow that a less expensive lawyer is not.

Another point to keep in mind is that lawyers, like all professionals, tend to specialize in one or two fields. A person certainly wouldn't go to a dentist for a stomach ache, or call the plumber if the lights went out, so why hire a civil lawyer for a draft case? You should make sure that the lawyer you hire knows a great deal about draft law. The best way to be sure of this is to hire a lawyer who handles a lot of draft cases. Such lawyers are likely to be well known to the draft counselors in their area.

Do **not** depend on father's lawyer just because he has always done well for father. After all, father isn't getting drafted, is he? The lawyer may be a real whiz at handling taxes and civil law suits, but he may know less about draft law than you do.

The decision of whether to accept or refuse induction is not simple, nor is it easy. There are a lot of things to be considered, and your final decision could affect your life for quite a while to come. It is unfortunate that such choices are forced on people, and yet the decision is there and cannot be ignored. You should decide well ahead of time what you are going to do if ordered for induction. A decision made in the heat of the moment is unlikely to be well thought out.

DRAFT CASES IN COURT

During the Vietnam era there was so much publicity given to draft cases in court, especially Supreme Court decisions, that many people began to think that going to court was one of the steps in appealing an unsatisfactory draft situation. The Selective Service Act makes it very clear that in most cases this cannot be done.[1] While it is possible to get a court injunction against the SS under certain conditions, and in rare cases it is even possible to have a federal court review your classification, the most common way to "take a case to court" is to be the defendant - to have the United States government bring charges for an alleged violation of the Selective Service law.

The usual charge landing people in court has been refusing induction, although people have also been taken to court for refusing to register, late registration, destroying draft board files, trashing draft boards, and so on. Since refusing induction is the most common charge, that is the one we will focus on in this chapter.

We should first take a moment to consider what it means to be a defendant in court. If it were possible to sue the SS, a person could bring suit any time he was displeased with his draft situation. If he lost in court, he would be no worse off than he was before the suit. Congress realized that, and realized what it meant in terms of bogging down the system and the courts. That is why the Selective Service Act is designed to prohibit suits against the SS.

As a defendant, you stand to lose a lot if your court case fails. In order to get to court, you first have to violate the law. Any violation of SS law carries a maximum penalty of five years in prison and/or a ten thousand dollar fine.[2] Taking a case to court is not a simple matter of filing suit against the SS. To get into court you have to bet up to five years of your life that you will win. I am a gambler, but at those stakes I am not about to bet unless I am pretty sure I have a winner.

Going to court almost always complicates a case, especially since the prosecutor may decide to charge you with every possible violation he can dig out of your file. For example, it may be that a man will be charged with refusing induction, and also with failure to register on time (because he registered two months late) and with failure to keep the system informed of a current address (because he moved and didn't tell them for a month). It is possible to be acquitted on the charge of refusing induction, but still be convicted on other charges. Because of the possibility of multiple charges being brought, it is usually best for you to try very hard to clear things up through the SS before it gets to the point of going to court. Usually a bit of effort, along with the attitude that you sincerely want to straighten things out through the system, will be enough to get what you want from the SS. Of course, there are times when no amount of effort seems to work, and a confrontation in court is the best or only choice you may have.

If you are going to end up in court, you probably will stand a much better chance of winning if you have a good draft lawyer handling your case. The court may offer free lawyers if you can't afford a private lawyer. In some courts a man may be allowed to choose the lawyer he wants to represent him, but in most cases getting a free, court-appointed lawyer means that you will have to accept whomever the court appoints. That is fine until you discover that the lawyer you have been given has never handled a draft case, right? In one case, a court-appointed lawyer actually talked his client into accepting induction rather than going into court, even though the man had a good defense, because the appointed lawyer did not know enough about draft law to spot the defense.

If you don't know a good draft lawyer, your draft counselor may be able to recommend someone. You might contact the local chapter of the National Lawyers Guild or the American Civil Liberties Union for referral to a draft law specalist. In many cases those groups can help you find an experienced draft lawyer even if you have but little money to pay.

There are three main lines of defense used in cases of refusing induction: (1) procedural errors, (2) ungranted classifications, and (3) challenging the constitutionality of the draft. There are pros and cons to each kind of defense, and many times more than one approach will be used in the same defense.

Procedural errors

Probably the most common defense used is that of procedural errors. Any time the SS takes action in processing a person toward induction, there are certain legal guidelines which must be followed. The processing procedures are defined in the Selective Service regulations and in the Registrant Processing Manual. These two documents are very lengthy and make boring reading, but they are cross-referenced, and may be helpful to anyone who thinks he may have spotted a procedural error.

Any time the SS fails to follow the correct processing procedure, the system has violated your rights under SS law, and has committed a procedural error. In cases where a procedural error has no bearing on your present draft situation, it is probably not useful as a defense. The courts usually hold that a procedural error must be prejudicial in order to give rise to a defense. But in many cases an error will have some bearing on the case and will be deemed to have prejudiced you. Since it takes many steps to process you for induction, especially assuming you requested some deferment or exemption, the SS has many opportunities to commit errors, and very often one error leads to another. Cases involving procedural errors seldom get as far as a full trial, although they may go to trial if there is a question of whether the action of the SS was legal, or whether an illegal act was prejudicial.

As an example of a procedural error which would raise a valid defense to a charge of refusing induction, let's say Jimmy Sarni submits a valid claim for conscientious objector status. The local board denies the claim and immediately orders him to report for induction. The order is illegal, since Jimmy must be allowed time in which to exercise his appeal rights. If Jimmy reports as ordered and refuses induction, the procedural error will act as a defense to the charge. However, it will not be a defense to some other unrelated charge, such as late registration.

Getting a bit more complex, let's say a man is assigned lottery number 152. During the year in which he turns twenty he has a dependency deferment. In December of that year the SS announces that draft calls are going only up to lottery number 150. On December 29 our man writes to his local board and informs them that his dependent has died. The following year he is placed into the First Priority Group, inductions go up to lottery number 285, and the man is ordered to report for induction. The order is illegal. Regardless of the man's deferment, the year he turned twenty was the year he was in the First Priority Group. Since his lottery number was not reached **that year**, he should have been placed into the Second Priority Group on January 1. Since no one was being called from the Second Priority Group, the procedural error was prejudicial and constitutes a valid defense to a charge of refusing induction. This is also know as an Order of Call defense.

Well before trial the United States Attorney's office reviews draft files to decide whether or not to pursue the case. If one or more prejudicial procedural errors are found, or if your lawyer contacts the US Attorney and points out procedural errors, the file may be sent back to the local board along with a letter explaining that the government chooses not to prosecute. The local board must then re-process you, starting from the point of the earliest procedural error. In many cases that means that the local board will reopen your classification, with the right to a personal appearance and a state appeal. Every once in a while when the SS has really botched a case, files have been known to mysteriously disappear.

Ungranted classification

The second type of defense involves an ungranted classification, or what is known as a "basis in fact" defense. There are times when a person feels that he is entitled to a certain classification, but for some reason the SS refuses to grant it to him. This is especially common with conscientious objector classifications, although it has happened with other classifications as well. After going through all available legal procedures - local board personal appearance, state appeal, and perhaps even a national appeal - a person may find himself still classified 1-A and facing an induction order. Many people in this circumstance have felt that they were being unjustly denied their legal right to a classification for which they were qualified, and rather than to allow the SS to break the law by denying them their legal right, have chosen to refuse induction.

It is sometimes possible to convince the local board that they have committed an error, and to persuade them to reopen your classification and reconsider it. Failing that, if you refuse induction it may be possible for your lawyer to convince the US Attorney that the local board erred, and to persuade the US Attorney not to prosecute and to send the file back to the local board with a letter recommending that your request be granted. Contact with the US Attorney won't always work, but is always worth a try.

If you end up raising the issue of your classification as a defense to a charge of refusing induction, the argument will be that the SS had no legal reason to classify you as eligible for induction in the first place.

For instance, if Brad Freeburg becomes a minister and requests a ministerial exemption (4-D) from his draft board, he has made a valid request. Say his board says that although he is an ordained minister in the Universal Life Church, he is not qualified for a 4-D classification because the Universal Life Church is not a recognized church. The board refuses to classify Brad 4-D for that reason, and so does the appeal board. Brad is issued an order to report for induction, and refuses induction.

In court Brad argues that SS regulations do not have a list of approved churches. To qualify for a 4-D exemption a man must simply be a full time minister of religion. Since Brad can prove that he serves a regular congregation of fifteen people, plus many more in his "street ministry", and that he spends an average of thirty hours a week acting as a minister, he feels qualified for a 4-D exemption. Further, he presented all of that information to the SS, but was denied an exemption by them.

Brad has a valid "basis in fact" defense.[3] The SS had no legal basis for denial of his claim, and therefore no basis in fact for his 1-A classification. Since it is illegal to order a person classified 4-D to report for induction, and since Brad has proved that he was in fact 4-D but for the board's errors, his induction order was illegal. You can't convict a man for refusing an illegal order.

The basis in fact defense has been most commonly raised in cases where claims of 1-O conscientious objector status have been denied. There are literally hundreds of reported court cases in this area alone. When denying a conscientious objector claim the SS is required to give reasons for denial.[4] However, there must be a basis in fact for its reasons.[5] The courts have reviewed SS reasoning in this area and set guidelines for local boards to follow.

One common reason for denying a conscientious objector claim is the board finding that the man does not sincerely hold his stated beliefs. However, such a finding may not rest on mere disbelief by the local board.[6] A failure to use appeals or obey the law is not enough to support a finding of insincerity.[7] "Late filing" of a claim does not support a finding of insincerity as long as the claim is filed in time for local board consideration.[8] A lack of formal religious training or failure to belong to an organized church can not be a basis for denying conscientious objector status.[9] The list of invalid reasons for denial goes on and on.

In court, the person you must convince is the judge. If he or she feels that the SS wrongfully denied a classification, you will be found not guilty and the matter will be referred back to the local board, perhaps with the judge's recommendation that the board grant the classification you want. The entire case may even be thrown out of court before the trial begins. It has happened that an informal meeting in the judge's chambers or a well prepared trial brief has resulted in the case never getting to the courtroom.

Of course, if the judge feels that a man is not qualified for the classification, that he did not do everything in his power to try to get the classification granted through the system, or that the SS reason for denial is sufficient, the man may be found guilty. If, for instance, a man submitted a conscientious objector claim, was reclassified

1-A, but never requested a local board personal appearance, or was turned down by the local board and did not appeal to the state appeal board, his chances in court are pretty bad.

The courts have consistently held since 1944 that in order for a basis in fact defense to be raised in court, a man must first have "exhausted his administrative remedies".[10] In other words, he must have used every available means to solve the problem through the system. Failure to appeal an unsatisfactory classification legally means that the man has accepted that classification. For that reason, he has no right to argue in court that he should be acquitted on the basis of an ungranted classification. If you plan to go to court over an ungranted classification, you should be very sure that you are qualified for that classification and that you have done everything in your power to get the classification granted by the SS.

In the past, the basis in fact defense has worked well in cases involving ungranted claims for conscientious objector status and for hardship deferments. However, it has not had a very good track record in the area of medical exemptions. The attitude of the courts seems to be that they will not act as "super draft boards" to determine a man's eligibility for a given classification, but are willing to review whether or not a local board determination rested on some ascertainable factual basis. Thus the courts will not find a man eligible for conscientious objector status, but will find that the reasons given by the SS for denial of a conscientious objector claim are invalid if there is no factual basis for the SS findings. In the area of medical exemption the courts have consistently refused to sit as AFEES examiners, and have almost always accepted the conclusion of the AFEES regarding a man's acceptability rather than to find that AFEES erred in finding a man acceptable. Because of this, a man whose ungranted classification is a 4-F exemption should not expect the same degree of success with his defense as the man whose ungranted classification is a 1-O or a 3-A.

Consititutionality

The third kind of defense is to challenge the constitutionality of the draft. While I personally feel strongly that the Selective Service System goes directly against the United States Constitution, it must be pointed out that this line of defense has never been successful. Various issues of constitutional magnitude - such as the power of the federal government to conscript, the power to draft people to fight in undeclared wars, the infringement upon freedom of religion or freedom of speech, the infringement upon freedom of association, the prohibition of involuntary servitude, and many other points - have been raised at one time or another, and have consistently lost.[11] This line of defense will almost certainly result in a person being found guilty, unless it is used along with another line of defense.

If you are strongly convinced that the government has no right to draft you, and if you are willing to face the probability of a conviction and possible prison sentence, you have my best wishes and firm support, but given the state of the law and the current attitude of the courts, I seriously doubt whether an attack on the constitutionality of the Selective Service System will prevail.

Other lines of defense

Some of the defenses used in traditional criminal cases, such as lack of intent, lack of knowledge, mistake of fact, and so on, have mostly been unsuccessful in Selective Service cases. As discussed in Chapter 11, a draft registrant has a legal duty to insure that all SS mail reaches him, and that all of his mail to the SS reaches the system. Because of those duties, along with the judicial presumption of administrative regularity (a presumption that the SS has done everything correctly) and the judicial presumption that SS mail which is sent out has been received, it is extremely difficult for a draft defendant to convince a judge or jury that he did not receive a particular order without also admitting that he violated his legal duty to keep the system informed of an address where mail would reach him.

In cases involving charges other than refusing induction or failure to report for induction - such as failure to register, late registration, failure to report a change of address, and so on - it is unlikely that a defense involving procedural errors or ungranted classification would be successful. Attorneys handling such cases should study the Selective Service Law Reporter Practice Manual, and also Veiluva, Registration And the Military Selective Service Act. These are available from CCCO, whose addresses appear in the back of this book.

Sentencing pratices

On the brighter side, not all men who violate the draft law have been prosecuted, not all men who have been prosecuted have been convicted, and not all men who have been convicted have been sentenced to prison.

During the Vietnam draft, and particularly in the later years of that draft, less than ten percent of the people who refused induction were actually prosecuted.[12] This low percentage was no doubt in direct relation to the upsurge in the number of men filing for deferments, exemptions, and conscientious objector status. By filing such claims men made use of their procedural rights under the draft law, and in doing so allowed local boards and appeal boards to make countless procedural errors and to provide innumerable faulty reasons for denial of claims. The system was so inept at processing men for induction that literally hundreds of thousands of men who refused induction had their files returned to the local boards for further processing.

However, even though nine cases out of ten were not prosecuted, this does not mean that only one in ten

could have been prosecuted. In many instances a man who had refused induction would find that he had virtually no defense to the charges. Rather than face an almost certain conviction and the possibility of a prison sentence, many thousands of men agreed to accept induction if re-ordered, or to enlist in order to avoid prosecution. Thus, while nine men out of ten were not prosecuted, far fewer actually succeeded in avoiding the draft and in avoiding prosecution. In reviewing the following statistics, bear in mind that not all men who had charges dropped or dismissed went free. Many of them had charges dismissed only upon a showing that they had enlisted or volunteered for induction.

During 1971 there were 2,973 men charged with violating the Selective Service Act. Of those men, 57% (1,701) had charges dismissed, 7% (217) were acquitted by a court trial, and another .6% (19) were acquitted by a jury. Roughly 35% of the men charged (1,036) were found guilty, either because they entered pleas of guilty or "no contest" (590) or because their defense failed and they were found guilty by a judge (350) or a jury (96).

Of the 1,036 men found guilty, only 377 were sentenced to prison: 79 received sentences of one year or less, 140 were given sentences of one to three years, 129 received sentences between three and five years, and 29 were sentenced to prison for five years or more. However, 63% of the men convicted (650) were given probation sentences and only nine had fines imposed. The average prison term that year was 29 months.[13]

Not surprisingly, sentencing practices have varied from court to court. In Maryland, for instance, 31 men were charged with draft law violations during fiscal year 1971, and 14 (45%) were convicted. By contrast, in the San Diego, California district court 63 men were charged with draft law violations and only 16 (25%) were found guilty. Average prison terms likewise varied from a low of 19.6 months in

Oregon to a high of 41.1 months in the courts serving Maryland, the Carolinas, Virginia and West Virginia.[14]

The legal problems of draft law violators do not end with the courts or the prisons. While practices vary from one state to the next, most states discriminate against convicted draft law violators, since they are felons. In some states, such as California, draft law violators do not lose their rights to vote, to practice law or medicine, or other rights. In other states, they lose it all.

In addition to the legal disabilities of a draft law conviction, it is also possible that a federal felony conviction on a man's record could cause employment problems. While some employers will look beyond the fact of conviction to see what charge a man was convicted of, many will treat all felons the same regardless of whether their crime was murder or refusing to murder.

In the past, draft law violators who were no longer of draft age have almost always been able to receive a Presidential pardon. Such a pardon usually will remove most or all of the restrictions on a man's rights resulting from a draft law conviction. But here again, practices vary from state to state, and from one employer to the next. Presidential pardons may be requested by filling out special forms addressed to the United States Pardon Attorney.

It is also possible for a draft violator who is not yet twenty-two years old at the time of his conviction to be sentenced under the Federal Youth Corrections Act.[15] Sentencing under that Act results in an indeterminate sentence of six months to six years, although most men in the past found that their sentence under the Youth Corrections Act worked out about the same as if they had been sentenced under the Selective Service Act. A man sentenced under the Youth Corrections Act may not have the same legal disabilities imposed upon him as a man sentenced under the Selective Service Act, and will usually find that employment problems are also lessened.

For many men the possibility of conviction will persuade them to do whatever they are ordered to do. For others, following their conscience is more important than following the law. No one should refuse induction thinking he can "get away with it," that he will "get off light," or that it is an "easy way out." But then again, a violation of the law, even with its penalties, may be easier to live with in later years than a violation of your principles.

APPENDIXES

A. ALIENS AND THE DRAFT

Citizens of a country other than the US, and all stateless persons, are classified as "aliens". Aliens are required to apply to the United States government for permission to enter this country, and that permission is generally given in the form of a "visa". With few exceptions, aliens who permanently enter the US are subject to the draft law. However, in some cases aliens are treated differently from US citizens. Also, because of the numerous regulations issued by the Department of State and the Immigration and Naturalization Service (INS), aliens may find their options under the draft law limited. On the other hand, there is a special draft deferment, class 4-C, which is available only to aliens and some dual citizens, and only under some circumstances.

Aliens are admitted to the US under several different kinds of visas. If an alien intends to settle in this country he will usually be admitted on a permanent resident visa (also called immigrant status.) Aliens may also be admitted on temporary visas which allow them to stay in the US for specific reasons, such as for visiting, study, diplomatic purposes, and so on.

In some cases Canadian and British subjects with homes in Canada or Bermuda, Mexican nationals, and many nationals from the Carribean area are admitted into the US as non-immigrants without visas. Their draft status is the same as if they were admitted on the type of visa appropriate to the purpose of their visit. In addition, certain refugees and others are admitted on "parole" or "conditional entry" status. In practice, the SS treats them as permanent residents.

Dual citizens - citizens of both the US and a foreign country - are recognized in the US only if entitled to both citizenships at birth. A US citizen who becomes a citizen of another country is considered to have renounced his US citizenship when accepting citizenship in another country, and is treated as an alien by the US government. Both are likely to be subject to the draft, either because of their US citizenship or as an alien residing in the US.

Aliens Who Need Not Register For The Draft

A non-immigrant alien, admitted to the US on a temporary visa, is not required to register for the draft.[1] The following groups are admitted on temporary visas:

1. **Tourists** and visitors for pleasure.
2. **Students** in full-time programs approved by the Attorney General and the Office of Education, and their spouses and minor children, as long as they continue as satisfactory students.
3. **Exchange program participants** under the Mutual Educational and Cultural Exchange Act, and their spouses and minor children, as long as they continue in such programs.
4. **Alien doctors** here as exchange visitors.
5. **Temporary or seasonal workers** who have entered the US under an agreement with a foreign government or agency, as long as they continue on the job.
6. **Foreign executives and technical personnel** of international corporations who enter the US temporarily to work for the same employers.
7. **Visitors for business**, including "treaty traders" - foreign businessmen and investors admitted under commercial treaties.

8. **Foreign press representatives** in the US temporarily for media activities.

9. **Officials** such as ambassadors, consuls, and other employees of foreign governments and of international public organizations, such as the United Nations. Representatives of foreign governments admitted without visas are also exempt from draft registration.

10. **Aliens in transit** through the US, crewmen, fiancees of US citizens allowed here 90 days in advance of marriage.

11. **Treaty aliens** are aliens from a country having a treaty with the US exempting aliens from military service, so long as not admitted on permanent resident status. There are fifteen treaty countries involved (see discussion on treaty aliens, below).

An alien in one of the above groups should retain an official document in his possession showing that he is exempt from draft registation. For most men admitted on the types of visas listed above, the visa itself or its equivalent should suffice. For foreign diplomats, the Department of State form will work. For certain temporary workers, an INS form will have been issued. Besides carrying documentation to protect against harrasment for non-registration, a person exempt from draft registration has no other draft liability unless he changes his status to a type requiring draft registration. Normally this happens only when someone admitted on a temporary visa gains permanent resident status or becomes an illegal alien.

Aliens With Selective Service Obligations

Any male alien admitted to the US who is not in one of the exempt groups listed above, and all illegal aliens, must register for the draft if in an age group where registration is required.[2] Immigrant aliens admitted to the US for permanent residence must register.

If an alien of draft age enters the US as a non-immigrant and then applies for permanent resident status, the INS sometimes requires him to register with the SS before the change of status is finally approved. Whether that happens or not, such a man is legally required to register.

Most permanent resident aliens are subject to almost the same rules regarding deferments, exemptions, and induction into the US military as US citizens. Like other registrants, aliens who must register are legally required to report address changes and other material changes in their status.[3] As currently written, the draft law provides that an alien may not be ordered for induction unless he has resided in the US for at least one year.[4] Thus, a permanent resident alien should be eligible for class 4-C during his first year in this country. But because many permanent resident aliens have spent their first year here on temporary visas or before becoming old enough to register for the draft, this provision does not affect them.

"Treaty Aliens" On Permanent Residence Visas

As noted above, the US has treaties with fifteen foreign countries. Under those treaties, aliens from those countries are exempt from military service while in this country. The fifteen countries are: Argentina, Austria, Costa Rica, China (Nationalist), Estonia, Honduras, Ireland, Italy, Latvia, Liberia, Norway, Paraguay, Spain, Switzerland and Yugoslavia. The Justice Department ruled many years ago that a permanent resident treaty alien must be allowed exemption from the draft in order to honor US treaty obligations.[5] The courts have upheld that view.[6]

Permanent Residents Eligible For Temporary Visas

A permanent resident alien may obtain a 4-C exemption if his work makes him eligible for a temporary visa as an official or employee of a foreign government or international organization, or a treaty trader. To obtain such an exemption, one must often sign a waiver of the legal privileges otherwise given to people in similar jobs.[7] However, one may keep the permanent resident status and future eligibility for US citizenship. In addition, any permanent resident alien who is eligible for a temporary status may apply for it at an INS office within the US. But when doing so, he must give up his permanent resident status. Those who do so may find it difficult or impossible to regain permanent resident status or to become citizens.

Deferments and Exemptions for Aliens

All aliens, whether permanent residents or non-immigrants, are eligible for the deferments and exemptions listed below:

4-A Exemption for Veterans This is available to any alien who has served at least twelve months' active duty in the armed forces of a country listed below.[8] He should get a certificate of proof, written in English, from his country's consulate or embassy.
Argentina, Australia, Belgium, Bolivia, Brazil, Canada, Chile, China (Nationalist), Columbia, Costa Rica, Denmark, Dominican Republic, Ecuador, El Salvador, France, Federal Republic of Germany, Greece, Guatemala, Haiti, Honduras, Iceland, Italy, Japan, South Korea, Luxembourg, Mexico, Netherlands, New Zealand, Nicaragua, Norway, Pakistan, Panama, Paraguay, Peru, Philippines, Portugal, Spain, Thailand, Turkey, United Kingdom (Britian), Uruguay, Venezuela.

4-C while outside the US Any alien who has registered with Selective Service is entitled to a 4-C exemption while outside the US, as long as he has not been issued an induction or alternate service order.[9] Any alien who is a permanent resident and plans to travel outside the

US and return during a time when draft boards are operating should establish his plans with the local board. Under INS law, any person who leaves or remains outside the US to avoid being drafted during a time of war or a Presidentially declared national emergency can later be barred from entry into the US, or can be deported.[10]

Special Problems of Aliens

An alien doctor admitted to the US on an immigrant visa is eligible for draft registration, and is also eligible for induction into the US military, up to age 35.[11] Alien doctors should also refer to Chapter 10 for information regarding the doctors' draft.

Aliens who are illegally inside the US face special problems. If the SS discovers illegal aliens, they are reported to INS. However, the SS considers an alien illegally in the US to still be eligible for induction, and could even issue him an induction order while waiting to see whether INS will start deportation proceedings. Refusal to respond to an induction order could lead to prosecution for violation of the draft law, although deportation is much more likely. An alien who has deportation proceedings pending against him should be rejected at the AFEES induction station. However, if the reason for deportation is draft evasion, he can be inducted if the INS is willing to drop deportation proceedings for that purpose.[12] Not a very pleasing set of alternatives.

An alien who is convicted under the Selective Service law is subject to deportation. Thus, refusal of induction could lead to deportation, either before or after serving a prison sentence. But a citizen of the United States who is convicted by a military court of desertion in time of war and is dishonorably discharged can no longer lose his United States citizenship,[13] as used to be the case.

It is up to the consular service of the State Department to issue visas and to interpret the "inadmissible classes" section of the immigration law. At the border and within the United States, an alien must deal with the Immigration and Naturalization Service. An immigration lawyer is often helpful, and is really necessary in cases involving deportation, private bills, and many other immigration matters.

Naturalization of Conscientious Objectors

The oath for aliens granted US citizenship has alternative clauses for conscientious objectors. The usual clause is an oath to "bear arms on behalf of the United States when required by law." But one may swear to "perform non-combatant service in the Armed Forces of the United States when required by law" or to "perform work of national importance under civilian direction when required by law." The two alternatives correspond to class 1-A-O and class 1-O conscientious objection standards. (See Chapter 6 for further information about conscientious objection.)

The INS will not allow an alien to use an alternative ctizenship oath unless it is satisfied that he or she meets the draft law definition of conscientious objection. So far as I know, few conscientious objectors meeting Selective Service requirements for recognition have been denied US citizenship in recent years.

B. COUNSELING AGENCIES

These agencies are in touch with draft counseling activities all across the nation. You can write to them for information about draft laws, forms or for referal to a draft counselor or lawyer in your vicinity.

CENTRAL COMMITTEE FOR CONSCIENTIOUS OBJECTORS (CCCO)
2208 South Street
Philadelphia, PA 19146
(215) 545-4626

or

1251 Second Avenue
San Francisco, CA 94122
(415) 566-0500
1-415-474-3002   *1-800-722-3538*

NATIONAL INTER-RELIGIOUS SERVICE BOARD FOR CONSCIENTIOUS OBJECTORS (NISBCO)
550 Washington Building
15th and New York Avenue NW
Washington, DC 20005

MIDWEST COMMITTEE FOR MILITARY & DRAFT COUNSELING
1006 Century Building
202 South State Street
Chicago, IL 60604
(312) 939-3349

C. MEDICAL STANDARDS

CHAPTER 2

MEDICAL FITNESS STANDARDS FOR APPOINTMENT, ENLISTMENT, AND INDUCTION

(Short Title: PROCUREMENT MEDICAL FITNESS STANDARDS)

Section I. GENERAL

2–1. Scope

This chapter sets forth the medical conditions and physical defects which are causes for rejection for military service in peacetime. For medical fitness standards during mobilization, see chapter 6.

2–2. Applicability

These standards apply to—

★*a.* Applicants for appointment as commissioned or warrant officers in the Active Army, Army National Guard, and Army Reserve. (Special categories of personnel, such as physicians, dentists, and other specialists, will be procured under standards prescribed by the Secretary of the Army in appropriate personnel procurement program directives.)

★*b.* Applicants for enlistment in the Active Army, Army National Guard, and Army Reserve. These standards are applicable until enlistees have completed 4 months of active duty or active duty for training for medical conditions or physical defects existing prior to original enlistment or induction. (See also AR 635-40, AR 635-200, AR 135-178, and NGR 135-178 for administrative procedure for separation for medically unfitting conditions that existed prior to service.)

★*c.* Applicants for reenlistment in the Active Army, Army National Guard, and Army Reserve after a period of more than 90 days has elapsed since discharge.

d. Applicants for the Army ROTC Scholarship Program, the Advanced Course Army ROTC, and other personnel procurement programs, other than induction for which these standards are prescribed.

★*e.* Retention of cadets of the United States Military Academy, students enrolled in the Uniformed Services University of Health Sciences, and the Army ROTC programs, except for such conditions that have been diagnosed since entrance into the Academy University or the ROTC programs. With respect to such conditions, upon recommendation of the Surgeon, United States Military Academy (for USMA cadets), or the Commanding General, United States Army Health Services Command (for ROTC cadets), the President, Uniformed Services University of Health Sciences (for students enrolled in that institution), the medical fitness standards of chapter 3 are applicable for retention in the Academy, the ROTC programs, and the University of Health Sciences, and entrance on active duty or active duty for training in a commissioned or enlisted status.

f. Registrants who undergo preinduction or induction medical examination, except medical and dental and allied medical specialists registrants who are to be evaluated under chapter 8.

g. Male applicants for enlistment in the US Air Force.

h. Male applicants for enlistment or reenlistment in the US Navy or Naval Reserve.

i. "Chargeable accessions" for enlistment in the US Marine Corps or Marine Corps Reserve.

2–1

208

Section III. BLOOD AND BLOOD-FORMING TISSUE DISEASES

2–4. Blood and Blood-Forming Tissue Diseases

The causes for rejection for appointment, enlistment and induction are—

a. Anemia:

(1) Blood less anemia—until both condition and basic cause are corrected.

(2) Deficiency anemia, not controlled by medication.

(3) Abnormal destruction of RBC's: Hemolytic anemia.

(4) Faulty RBC construction: Hereditary hemolytic anemia, thallassemia, and sickle cell-lanemia.

(5) Myelophthisic anemia: Myelomatosis, leukemia, Hodgkin's disease.

(6) Primary refractory anemia: Aplastic anemia, DiGuglielmo's syndrome.

b. Hemorrhagic states:

(1) Due to changes in coagulation system (hemophilia, etc.).

2–2.01

(2) Due to platelet deficiency.

(3) Due to vascular instability.

c. Leukopenia, chronic or recurrent, associated with increased susceptibility to infection.

d. Myeloproliferative disease (other than leukemia):

(1) **Myelofibrosis.**

(2) **Megakaryocytic myelosis.**

(3) **Polycythemia vera.**

e. Splenomegaly until the cause is remedied.

f. Thromboembolic disease except for acute, nonrecurrent conditions.

Section II. ABDOMEN AND GASTROINTESTINAL SYSTEM

2–3. Abdominal Organs and Gastrointestinal System

The causes for rejection for appointment, enlistment, and induction are—

a. *Cholecystectomy,* sequelae of, such as postoperative stricture of the common bile duct, reforming of stones in hepatic or common bile ducts, or incisional hernia, or postcholecystectomy syndrome when symptoms are so severe as to interfere with normal performance of duty.

b. *Cholecystitis,* acute or chronic, with or without cholelithiasis, if diagnosis is confirmed by usual laboratory procedures or authentic medical records.

c. *Cirrhosis* regardless of the absence of manifestations such as jaundice, ascites or known esophageal varices, abnormal liver function tests with or without history of chronic alcoholism.

d. *Fistula* in ano.

e. *Gastritis,* chronic hypertrophic, severe.

f. *Hemorrhoids.*

(1) External hemorrhoids producing marked symptoms.

(2) Internal hemorrhoids, if large or accompanied with hemorrhage or protruding intermittently or constantly.

g. *Hepatitis* within the preceding 6 months, or persistence of symptoms after a reasonable period of time with objective evidence of impairment of liver function.

h. *Hernia:*

(1) Hernia other than small asymptomatic umbilical or hiatal.

(2) History of operation for hernia within the preceding 60 days.

i. *Intestinal obstruction* or authenticated history of more than one episode, if either occurred during the preceding 5 years or if resulting condition remains which produces significant symptoms or requires treatment.

j. *Megacolon* of more than minimal degree;

diverticulitis, *regional enteritis* and *ulcerative colitis. Irritable colon* of more than moderate degree.

k. *Pancreas,* acute or chronic disease of, if proven by laboratory tests, or authenticated medical records.

l. *Rectum,* stricture or prolapse of.

m. *Resection, gastric or of bowel,* or *gastroenterostomy;* however minimal intestinal resection in infancy or childhood *(for example:* for intussusception or pyloric stenosis) is acceptable if the individual has been asymptomatic since the resection and if surgical consultation (to include upper and lower gastrointestinal series) gives complete clearance.

n. *Scars.*

(1) Scars, abdominal, regardless of cause, which show hernial bulging or which interfere with movements.

(2) Scar pain associated with disturbance of function of abdominal wall or contained viscera.

o. *Sinuses* of the abdominal wall.

p. *Splenectomy,* except when accomplished for the following:

(1) Trauma.

(2) Causes unrelated to diseases of the spleen.

(3) Hereditary spherocytosis.

(4) Disease involving the spleen when followed by correction of the condition for a period of at least 2 years.

q. *Tumors.* See paragraphs 2–40 and 2–41.

r. *Ulcer:*

(1) Ulcer of the stomach or duodenum if diagnosis is confirmed by X-ray examination, or authenticated history thereof.

(2) Authentic history of surgical operation(s) for gastric or duodenal ulcer.

s. *Other* congenital or acquired abnormalities and defects which preclude satisfactory performance of military duty or which require frequent and prolonged treatment.

Section IV. DENTAL

2-5. Dental

The causes for rejection for appointment, enlistment, and induction are—

a. Diseases of the jaws or associated tissues which are not easily remediable and which will incapacitate the individual or prevent the satisfactory performance of military duty.

b. Malocclusion, severe, which interferes with the mastication of a normal diet.

c. Oral tissues, extensive loss of, in an amount that would prevent replacement of missing teeth with a satisfactory prosthetic appliance.

d. Orthodontic appliances. See special administrative criteria in paragraph 7-12. ✱

e. Relationship between the mandible and maxilla of such a nature as to preclude future satisfactory prosthodontic replacement.

Section V. EARS AND HEARING

2-6. Ears

The causes for rejection for appointment, enlistment, and induction are—

a. Auditory canal:
   (1) Atresia or severe stenosis of the external auditory canal.
   (2) Tumors of the external auditory canal except mild exostoses.
   (3) Severe external otitis, acute or chronic.

b. Auricle: Agenesis, severe; or severe traumatic deformity, unilateral or bilateral.

c. Mastoids:
   (1) Mastoiditis, acute or chronic.
   (2) Residual or mastoid operation with marked external deformity which precludes or interferes with the wearing of a gas mask or helmet.
   (3) Mastoid fistula.

d. Meniere's syndrome.

e. Middle ear:
   (1) Acute or chronic suppurative otitis media. Individuals with a recent history of acute suppurative otitis media will not be accepted unless the condition is healed and a sufficient interval of time subsequent to treatment has elapsed to insure that the disease is in fact not chronic.
   (2) Adhesive otitis media associated with hearing level by audiometric test of 20 db or more average for the speech frequencies (500, 1000, and 2000 cycles per second) in either ear regardless of the hearing level in the other ear.

   (3) Acute or chronic serous otitis media.
   (4) Presence of attic perforation in which presence of cholesteatoma is suspected.
   (5) Repeated attacks of catarrhal otitis media; intact greyish, thickened drum(s).

f. Tympanic membrane:
   ★(1) Any perforation of the tympanic membrane.
   (2) Severe scarring of the tympanic membrane associated with hearing level by audiometric test of 20 db or more average for the speech frequencies (500, 1000, and 2000 cycles per second) in either ear regardless of the hearing level in the other ear.

g. Other diseases and defects of the ear which obviously preclude satisfactory performance of duty or which require frequent and prolonged treatment.

2-7. Hearing

(See also para. 2-6.)

The cause for rejection for appointment, enlistment, and induction is—

Hearing acuity level by audiometric testing (regardless of conversational or whispered voice hearing acuity) greater than that described in table I, appendix II. There is no objection to conducting the whispered voice test or the spoken voice test as a preliminary to conducting the audiometric hearing test.

*see page 12

2-3

211

Section VI. ENDOCRINE AND METABOLIC DISORDERS

2–8. Endocrine and Metabolic Disorders

The causes for rejection for appointment, enlistment, and induction are—

a. Adrenal gland, malfunction of, of any degree.

b. Cretinism.

c. Diabetes insipidus.

d. Diabetes mellitus.

e. Gigantism or acromegaly.

f. Glycosuria, persistent, regardless of cause.

g. Goiter.

(1) Simple goiter with definite pressure symptoms or so large in size as to interfere with the wearing of a military uniform or military equipment.

(2) *Thyrotoxicosis.*

h. Gout.

i. Hyperinsulinism, confirmed, symptomatic.

j. Hyperparathyroidism and *hypoparathyroidism.*

k. Hypopituitarism, severe.

l. Myxedema, spontaneous or postoperative (with clinical manifestations and not based solely on low basal metabolic rate).

m. Nutritional deficiency diseases (including sprue, beriberi, pellagra, and scurvy) which are more than mild and not readily remediable or in which permanent pathological changes have been established.

n. Other endocrine or metabolic disorders which obviously preclude satisfactory performance of duty or which require frequent and prolonged treatment.

Section VII. EXTREMITIES

2–9. Upper Extremities

(See para 2–11.)

The causes for rejection for appointment, enlistment, and induction are—

★*a. Limitation of motion.* An individual will be considered unacceptable if the joint ranges of motion are less than the measurements listed below (TM 8–640).

(1) *Shoulder.*

(*a*) Forward elevation to 90°.

(*b*) Abduction to 90°.

(2) *Elbow.*

(*a*) Flexion to 100°.

(*b*) Extension to 15°.

(3) *Wrist.* A total range of 15° (extension plus flexion).

(4) *Hand.*

(*a*) Pronation to the first quarter of normal arc.

(*b*) Supination to the first quarter of the normal arc.

(5) *Fingers.* Inability to clench first, pick up a pin or needle, and grasp an object.

b. Hand and fingers.

(1) Absence (or loss) of more than ⅓ of the distal phalanx of either thumb.

(2) Absence (or loss) of distal and middle phalanx of an index, middle or ring finger of either hand irrespective of the absence (or loss) of little finger.

(2.1) Absence of more than the distal phalanx of any two of the following fingers, index, middle finger or ring finger, of either hand.

(3) Absence of hand or any portion thereof except for fingers as noted above.

(4) Hyperdactylia.

(5) Scars and deformities of the fingers and/or hand which impair circulation, are symptomatic, are so disfiguring as to make the individual objectionable in ordinary social relationships, or which impair normal function to such a degree as to interfere with the satisfactory performance of military duty.

c. Wrist, forearm, elbow, arm, and shoulder. Healed disease or injury of wrist, elbow, or shoulder with residual weakness or symptoms of such a degree as to preclude satisfactory performance of duty.

2–10. Lower Extremities

(See para 2–11.)

The causes for rejection for appointment, enlistment, and induction are—

2–4

★*a. Limitation of motion.* An individual will be considered unacceptable if the joint ranges of motion are less than the measurements listed below (TM 8-640).

(1) *Hip.*
   (*a*) Flexion to 90°.
   (*b*) Extension to 10° (beyond 0).
(2) *Knee.*
   (*a*) Full extension.
   (*b*) Flexion to 90°.
(3) *Ankle.*
   (*a*) Dorsiflexion to 10°.
   (*b*) Plantar flexion to 10°.
(4) *Toes.* Stiffness which interferes with walking, marching, running, or jumping.

b. Foot and ankle.

(1) Absence of one or more small toes of one or both feet, if function of the foot is poor or running or jumping is precluded, or absence of foot or any portion thereof except for toes as noted herein.

(2) Absence (or loss) of great toe(s) or loss of dorsal flexion thereof if function of the foot is impaired.

(3) Claw toes precluding the wearing of combat service boots.

(4) Clubfoot.

(5) Flatfoot, pronounced cases, with decided eversion of the foot and marked bulging of the inner border, due to inward rotation of the astragalus, regardless of the presence or absence of symptoms.

(6) Flatfoot, spastic.

(7) Hallux valgus, if severe and associated with marked exostosis or bunion.

(8) Hammer toe which interferes with the wearing of combat service boots.

(9) Healed disease, injury, or deformity including hyperdactylia which precludes running, is accompanied by disabling pain, or which prohibits wearing of combat service boots.

(10) Ingrowing toe nails, if severe, and not remediable.

(11) Obliteration of the transverse arch associated with permanent flexion of the small toes.

(12) Pes cavus, with contracted plantar fascia, dorsiflexed toes, tenderness under the metatarsal heads, and callosity under the weight bearing areas.

c. Leg, knee, thigh, and hip.

(1) Dislocated semilunar cartilage, loose or foreign bodies within the knee joint, or history of surgical correction of same if—

   (*a*) Within the preceding 6 months.

   (*b*) Six months or more have elapsed since operation without recurrence, and there is instability of the knee ligaments in lateral or anteroposterior directions in comparison with the normal knee or abnormalities noted on X-ray, there is significant atrophy or weakness of the thigh musculature in comparison with the normal side, there is not acceptable active motion in flexion and extension, or there are other symptoms of internal derangement.

(2) Authentic history or physical findings of an unstable or internally deranged joint causing disabling pain or seriously limiting function. Individuals with verified episodes of buckling or locking of the knee who have not undergone satisfactory surgical correction or if, subsequent to surgery, there is evidence of more than mild instability of the knee ligaments in lateral and anteroposterior directions in comparison with the normal knee, weakness or atrophy of the thigh musculature in comparison with the normal side, or if the individual requires medical treatment of sufficient frequency to interfere with the performance of military duty.

d. General.

(1) Deformities of one or both lower extremities which have interfered with function to such a degree as to prevent the individual from following a *physically active* vocation in civilian life or which would interefere with the satisfactory completion of prescribed training and performance of military duty.

(2) Diseases or deformities of the hip, knee, or ankle joint which interfere with walking, running, or weight bearing.

(3) Pain in the lower back or leg which is intractable and disabling to the degree of interfering with walking, running, and weight bearing.

(4) Shortening of a lower extremity resulting in any limp of noticeable degree.

2-5

2–11. Miscellaneous
(See also para 2–9 and 2–10.)
The causes for rejection for appointment, enlistment, and induction are—

a. Arthritis.

(1) Active or subacute arthritis, including Marie-Strumpell type.

(2) Chronic osteoarthritis or traumatic arthritis of isolated joints of more than minimal degree, which has interfered with the following of a physically active vocation in civilian life or which precludes the satisfactory performance of military duty.

(3) Documented clinical history of rheumatoid arthritis.

(4) Traumatic arthritis of a major joint of more than minimal degree.

b. Disease of any bone or joint, healed, with such resulting deformity or rigidity that function is impaired to such a degree that it will interfere with military service.

c. Dislocation, old unreduced; substantiated history of recurrent dislocations of major joints; instability of a major joint, symptomatic and more than mild; or if, subsequent to surgery, there is evidence of more than mild instability in comparison with the normal joint, weakness or atrophy in comparison with the normal side, or if the individual requires medical treatment of sufficient frequency to interfere with the performance of military duty.

d. Fractures.

(1) Malunited fractures that interfere significantly with function.

(2) Ununited fractures.

(3) Any old or recent fracture in which a plate, pin, or screws were used for fixation and left in place and which may be subject to easy trauma, i.e., as a plate tibia, etc.

e. Injury of a bone or joint within the preceding 6 weeks, without fracture or dislocation, of more than a minor nature.

f. Muscular paralysis, contracture, or atrophy, if progressive or of sufficient degree to interfere with military service.

f.1. Myotonia congenita. Confirmed.

g. Osteomyelitis, active or recurrent, of any bone or substantiated history of osteomyelitis of any of the long bones unless successfully treated 2 or more years previously without subsequent recurrence or disqualifying sequelae as demonstrated by both clinical and X-ray evidence.

h. Osteoporosis.

i. Scars, extensive, deep, or adherent, of the skin and soft tissues or neuromas of an extremity which are painful, which interfere with muscular movements, which preclude the wearing of military equipment, or that show a tendency to break down.

j. Chondromalacia, manifested by verified history of joint effusion, interference with function, or residuals from surgery.

Section VIII. EYES AND VISION

2–12. Eyes
The causes for rejection for appointment, enlistment, and induction are—

a. Lids.

(1) Blepharitis, chronic more than mild. Cases of acute blepharitis will be rejected until cured.

(2) Blepharospasm.

(3) Dacryocystitis, acute or chronic.

(4) Destruction of the lids, complete or extensive, sufficient to impair protection of the eye from exposure.

(5) Disfiguring cicatrices and adhesions of the eyelids to each other or to the eyeball.

(6) Growth or tumor of the eyelid other than small early basal cell tumors of the eyelid, which can be cured by treatment, and small nonprogressive asymptomatic benign lesions. See also paragraphs 2–40 and 2–41.

(7) Marked inversion or eversion of the eyelids sufficient to cause unsightly appearance or watering of eyes (entropion or ectropion).

(8) Lagophthalmos.

(9) Ptosis interfering with vision.

(10) Trichiasis, severe.

b. *Conjunctiva.*

(1) Conjunctivitis, chronic, including vernal catarrh and trachoma. Individuals with acute conjunctivitis are unacceptable until the condition is cured.

(2) Pterygium:

(a) Pterygium recurring after three operative procedures.

(b) Pterygium encroaching on the cornea in excess of 3 millimeters or interfering with vision.

c. *Cornea.*

(1) Dystrophy, corneal, of any type including keratoconus of any degree.

(2) Keratitis, acute or chronic.

(3) Ulcer, corneal; history of recurrent ulcers or corneal abrasions (including herpetic ulcers).

★(4) Vascularization or opacification of the cornea from any cause which is progressive or reduces vision below the standards prescribed in paragraph 2–13.

d. *Uveal tract.* Inflammation of the uveal tract except healed traumatic choroiditis.

e. *Retina.*

(1) Angiomatoses, phakomatoses, retinal cysts, and other congenito-hereditary conditions that impair visual function.

(2) Degenerations of the retina to include macular cysts, holes, and other degenerations (hereditary or acquired degenerative changes) and other conditions affecting the macula. All types of pigmentary degenerations (primary and secondary).

(3) Detachment of the retina or history of surgery for same.

(4) Inflammation of the retina (retinitis or other inflammatory conditions of the retina 'to include Coat's disease, diabetic retinopathy, Eales' disease, and retinitis proliferans).

f. *Optic nerve.*

(1) Congenito-hereditary conditions of the optic nerve or any other central nervous system pathology affecting the efficient function of the optic nerve.

(2) Optis neuritis, neuroretinitis, or secondary optic atrophy resulting therefrom or document history of attacks of retrobulbar neuritis.

(3) Optic atrophy (primary or secondary).

(4) Papilledema.

g. *Lens.*

(1) Aphakia (unilateral or bilateral).

(2) Dislocation, partial or complete, of a lens.

(3) Opacities of the lens which interfere with vision or which are considered to be progressive.

h. *Ocular mobility and motility.*

(1) Diplopia, documented, constant or intermittent from any cause or of any degree interfering with visual function (i.e., may suppress).

(2) Diplopia, monocular, documented, interfering with visual function.

(3) Nystagmus, with both eyes fixing, congenital or acquired.

(4) Strabismus of 40 prism diopters or more, uncorrectable by lenses to less than 40 diopters.

(5) Strabismus of any degree accompanied by documented diplopia.

(6) Strabismus, surgery for the correction of, within the preceding 6 months.

i. *Miscellaneous defects and diseases.*

(1) Abnormal conditions of the eye or visual fields due to diseases of the central nervous system.

(2) Absence of an eye.

(3) Asthenopia severe.

(4) Exophthalmos, unilateral or bilateral

(5) Glaucoma, primary or secondary

(6) Hemianopsia of any type.

(7) Loss of normal pupillary reflex reactions to light or accommodation to distance or Adies syndrome.

(8) Loss of visual fields due to organic disease.

(9) Night blindness associated with objective disease of the eye. Verified congenital night blindness.

(10) Residuals of old contusions, lacera-

2–7

tions, penetrations, etc., which impair visual function required for satisfactory performance of military duty.

(11) Retained intra-ocular foreign body.

(12) Tumors. See *a*(6) above and paragraphs 2–40 and 2–41.

(13) Any organic disease of the eye or adnexa not specified above which threatens continuity of vision or impairment of visual function.

2–13. Vision

The causes for medical rejection for appointment, enlistment, and induction are listed below. The special administrative criteria for officer assignment to Armor, Artillery, Infantry, Corps of Engineers, Signal Corps, and Military Police Corps are listed in paragraph 7–15.

★*a. Distant visual acuity.* Distant visual acuity of any degree which does correct with spectacle lenses to at least one of the following:

(1) 20/40 in one eye and 20/70 in the other eye.

(2) 20/30 in one eye and 20/100 in the other eye.

(3) 20/20 in one eye and 20/400 in the other eye.

b. Near visual acuity. Near visual acuity of any degree which does not correct to at least J–6 in the better eye.

c. Refractive error. Any degree of refractive error in spherical equivalent of over −8.00 or +8.00; or if ordinary spectacles cause discomfort by reason of ghost images, prismatic displacement, etc.; or if an ophthalmological consultation reveals a condition which is disqualifying.

d. Contact lens. Complicated cases requiring contact lens for adequate correction of vision as keratoconus, corneal scars, and irregular astigmatism.

Section IX. GENITOURINARY SYSTEM

2–14. Genitalia

(See also para 2–40 and 2–41.)

The causes for rejection for appointment, enlistment, and induction are—

a. Bartholinitis, Bartholin's cyst.

b. Cervicitis, acute or chronic manifested by leukorrhea.

c. Dysmenorrhea, incapacitating to a degree which necessitates recurrent absences of more than a few hours from routine activities.

d. Endometriosis, or confirmed history thereof.

e. Hermaphroditism.

f. Memopausal syndrome, either physiologic or artificial if manifested by more than mild constitutional or mental symptoms, or artificial menopause if less than 13 months have elapsed since cessation of menses. In all cases of artificial menopause, the clinical diagnosis will be reported; if accomplished by surgery, the pathologic report will be obtained and recorded.

g. Menstrual cycle, irregularities of, including menorrhagia, if excessive; metrorrhagia; polymenorrhea; amenorrhea, except as noted in *f* above.

h. New growths of the internal or external genitalia except single uterine fibroid, subser-

2–8

216

ous, asymptomatic, less than 3 centimeters in diameter, with no general enlargement of the uterus. See also paragraphs 2-40 and 2-41.

i. Oophoritis, acute or chronic.

j. Ovarian cysts, persistent and considered to be of clinical significance.

k. Pregnancy.

l. Salpingitis, acute or chronic.

m. Testicle(s). (See also para 2-40 and 2-41.)

(1) Absence or nondescent of both testicles.

(2) Undiagnosed enlargement or mass of testicle or epididymis.

(3) Undescended testicle.

n. Urethritis, acute or chronic, other than gonorrheal urethritis without complications.

o. Uterus.

(1) Cervical polyps, cervical ulcer, or marked erosion.

(2) Endocervicitis, more than mild.

(3) Generalized enlargement of the uterus due to any cause.

(4) Malposition of the uterus if more than mildly symptomatic.

p. Vagina.

(1) Congenital abnormalities or severe lacerations of the vagina.

(2) Vaginitis, acute or chronic, manifested by leukorrhea.

q. Varicocele or hydrocele, if large or painful.

r. Vulva.

(1) Leukoplakia.

(2) Vulvitis, acute or chronic.

s. Major abnormalities and defects of the genitalia such as a change of sex, a history thereof, or complications (adhesions, disfiguring scars, etc.) residual to surgical correction of these conditions.

2-15. Urinary System

(See para 2-8, 2-40, and 2-41).
The causes for rejection for appointment, enlistment, and induction are—

a. Albuminuria if persistent or recurrent including so-called orthostatic or functional albuminuria.

b. Cystitis, chronic. Individuals with acute cystitis are unacceptable until the condition is cured.

c. Enuresis determine to be a symptom of an organic defect not amenable to treatment. (See also para 2-34c.)

d. Epispadias or hypospadias when accompanied by evidence of infection of the urinary tract or if clothing is soiled when voiding.

e. Hematuria, cylindruria, or other findings indicative of renal tract disease.

f. Incontinence of urine.

g. Kidney.

(1) Absence of one kidney, regardless of cause.

(2) Acute or chronic infections of the kidney.

(3) Cystic or polycystic kidney, confirmed history of.

(4) Hydronephrosis or pyonephrosis.

(5) Nephritis, acute or chronic.

(6) Pyelitis, pyelonephritis.

h. Penis, amputation of, if the resulting stump is insufficient to permit micturition in a normal manner.

i. Peyronie's disease.

j. Prostate gland, hyperthrophy of, with urinary retention.

k. Renal calculus.

(1) Substantiated history of bilateral renal calculus at any time.

(2) Verified history of renal calculus at any time with evidence of stone formation within the preceding 12 months, current symptoms or positive X-ray for calculus.

l. Skeneitis.

m. Urethra.

(1) Stricture of the urethra.

(2) Urethritis, acute or chronic, other than gonorrheal urethritis without complications.

n. Urinary fistula.

o. Other diseases and defects of the urinary system which obviously preclude satisfactory performance of duty or which require frequent and prolonged treatment.

Section X. HEAD AND NECK

2–16. Head

The causes for rejection for appointment, enlistment, and induction are—

a. Abnormalities which are apparently temporary in character resulting from recent injuries until a period of 3 months has elapsed. These include severe contusions and other wounds of the scalp and cerebral concussion. See paragraph 2–31.

b. Deformities of the skull in the nature of depressions, exostoses, etc., of a degree which would prevent the individual from wearing a gas mask or military headgear.

c. Deformities of the skull of any degree associated with evidence of disease of the brain, spinal cord, or peripheral nerves.

d. Depressed fractures near central sulcus with or without convulsive seizures.

e. Loss or congenital absence of the bony substance of the skull not successfully corrected by reconstructive material:

(1) All cases involving absence of the bony substance of the skull which have been corrected but in which the defect is in excess of 1 square inch or the size of a 25 cent piece, will be referred to The Surgeon General together with a report of consultation;

(2) The report of consultation will include an evaluation of any evidence of alteration of brain function in any of its several spheres, i.e., intelligence, judgment, perception, behavior, motor control and sensory function as well as any evidence of active bone disease or other related complications. Current X-rays and other pertinent laboratory data will accompany such a report of consultation.

f. Unsightly deformities, such as large birthmarks, large hairy moles, extensive scars and mutilations due to injuries or surgical operations; ulcerations; fistulae, atrophy, or paralysis of part of the face or head.

2–17. Neck

The causes for rejection for appointment, enlistment, and induction are—

a. Cervical ribs if symptomatic, or so obvious that they are found on routine physical examination. (Detection based primarily on X-ray is not considered to meet this criterion.)

b. Congenital cysts of branchial cleft origin or those developing from the remnants of the thyroglossal duct, with or without fistulous tracts.

c. Fistula, chronic draining, of any type.

★*d.* (Deleted)

e. Nonspastic contraction of the muscles of the neck or cicatricial contracture of the neck to the extent that it interferes with the wearing of a uniform or military equipment or so disfiguring as to make the individual objectionable in common social relationships.

f. Spastic contraction of the muscles of the neck, persistent, and chronic.

g. Tumor of thyroid or other structures of the neck. See paragraphs 2–40 and 2–41.

Section XI. HEART AND VASCULAR SYSTEM

2–18. Heart

The causes for rejection for appointment, enlistment, and induction are—

a. All organic valvular diseases of the heart, including those improved by surgical procedures.

b. Coronary artery disease or myocardial infarction, old or recent or true angina pectoris, at any time.

c. Electrocardiographic evidence of major arrhythmias such as—

(1) Atrial tachycardia, flutter, or fibrillation, ventricular tachycardia or fibrillation.

(2) Conduction defects such as first degree atrio-ventricular block and right bundle branch block. (These conditions occurring as isolated findings are not unfitting when cardiac evaluation reveals no cardiac disease.)

(3) Left bundle branch block, 2d and 3d degree AV block.

(4) Unequivocal electrocardiographic evidence of old or recent myocardial infarction; coronary insufficiency at rest or after stress; or evidence of heart muscle disease.

d. Hypertrophy or dilatation of the heart as evidenced by clinical examination or roentgenographic examination and supported by electrocardiographic examination. Care should be taken to distinguish abnormal enlargement from increased diastolic filling as seen in the well conditioned subject with a sinus bradycardia. Cases of enlarged heart by X-ray not supported by electrocardiographic examination will be forwarded to The Surgeon General for evaluation.

e. Myocardial insufficiency (congestive circulatory failure, cardiac decompensation) obvious or covert, regardless of cause.

f. Paroxysmal tachycardia within the preceding 5 years, or at any time if recurrent or disabling or if associated with electrocardiographic evidence of accelerated A-V conduction (Wolff-Parkinson White).

★*g. Pericarditis; endocarditis; or myocarditis*, history or finding of, except for a history of a single acute idiopathic or coxsackie pericarditis with no residuals, or tuberculous pericarditis adequately treated with no residuals and inactive for 2 years.

h. Tachycardia persistent with a resting pulse rate of 100 or more, regardless of cause.

2–19., Vascular System

The causes for rejection for appointment, enlistment, and induction are—

a. Congenital or acquired lesions of the aorta and major vessels, such as syphilitic aortitis, demonstrable atherosclerosis which interferes with circulation, congenital or acquired

dilation of the aorta (especially if associated with other features of Marfan's syndrome), and pronounced dilatation of the main pulmonary artery.

b. Hypertension evidenced by preponderant blood pressure readings of 150-mm or more systolic in an individual over 35 years of age or preponderant readings of 140-mm or more systolic in an individual 35 years of age or less. Preponderant diastolic pressure over 90-mm diastolic is cause for rejection at any age.

c. Marked circulatory instability as indicated by orthostatic hypotension, persistent tachycardia, severe peripheral vasomotor disturbances and sympatheticotonia.

d. Peripheral vascular disease including Raynaud's phenomena, Buerger's disease (thromboangiitis obliterans), erythromelalgia, arteriosclerotic and diabetic vascular diseases. Special tests will be employed in doubtful cases.

e. Thrombophlebitis.

(1) History of thrombophlebitis with persistent thrombus or evidence of circulatory obstruction or deep venous incompetence in the involved veins.

(2) Recurrent thrombophlebitis.

f. Varicose veins, if more than mild, or if associated with edema, skin ulceration, or residual scars from ulceration.

2–20. Miscellaneous

The causes for rejection for appointment, enlistment, and induction are—

c. Aneurysm of the heart or major vessel, congenital or acquired.

b. History and evidence of a congenital abnormality which has been treated by surgery but with residual abnormalities or complications, for example: Patent ductus arteriosus with residual cardiac enlargement or pulmonary hypertension; resection of a coarctation of the aorta without a graft when there are other cardiac abnormalities or complications; closure of a secundum type artrial septal defect when there are residual abnormalities or complications.

c. Major congenital abnormalities and defects by the heart and vessels unless satisfactorily corrected without residuals or complications. Uncom-

2–11

plicated dextrocardia and other minor asymptomatic anomalies are acceptable.

d. *Substantiated history of rheumatic fever or*

chorea within the previous 2 years, recurrent attacks of rheumatic fever or chorea at any time, or with evidence of residual cardiac damage.

Section XII. HEIGHT, WEIGHT, AND BODY BUILD

2–21. Height

The causes for rejection for appointment, enlistment, and induction are—

a. *For appointment.*

(1) *Men.* Regular Army—Height below 66 inches or over 80 inches. (See administrative criteria in para 7–13.) Other—Height below 60 inches or over 80 inches.

(2) *Women.* Height below 58 inches or over 72 inches.

b. *For enlistments and induction.*

(1) *Men.* Height below 60 inches or over 80 inches for Army and Air Force.

(2) *Men.* Height below 60 inches and over 78 inches for Navy and Marine Corps.

(3) *Women.* Height below 58 inches or over 72 inches.

2–22. Weight

The causes for rejection for appointment, enlistment, and induction are—

a. *Weight related to height* which is below the minimum shown in table I, appendix III for men and table II, appendix III for women.

b. *Weight related to age and height* which is in

excess of the maximum shown in table I, appendix III for men and table II, appendix III for women. See chapter 7 for special requirements pertaining to maximum weight standards applicable to women enlisting for and commissioned from Army Student Nurse and Army Student Dietician Programs.

2–23. Body Build

The causes for rejection for appointment, enlistment, and induction are—

a. *Congenital malformation of bones and joints.* (See para 2–9, 2–10, and 2–11.)

b. *Deficient muscular development* which would interfere with the completion of required training.

c. *Evidences of congenital asthenia* (slender bones; weak thorax; visceroptosis; severe, chronic constipation; or "drop heart" if marked in degree).

d. *Obesity.* Even though the individual's weight is within the maximum shown in table I or II, as appropriate, appendix III, he will be reported as medically unacceptable when the medical examiner considers that the individual's weight in relation to the bony structure and musculature, constitutes obesity of such a degree as to interfere with the satisfactory completion of prescribed training.

Section XIII. LUNGS AND CHEST WALL

2–24. General

The following conditions are causes for rejection for appointment, enlistment and induction until further study indicates recovery without disqualifying sequelae:

a. *Abnormal elevation of the diaphragm* on either side.

b. *Acute abscess* of the lung.

c. *Acute bronchitis* until the condition is cured.

d. *Acute fibrinous pleurisy,* associated with acute nontuberculous pulmonary infection.

e. *Acute mycotic disease* of the lung such as coccidioidomycosis and histoplasmosis.

f. *Acute nontuberculous pneumonia.*

g. *Foreign body in trachea or bronchus.*

h. *Foreign body of the chest wall* causing symptoms.

i. *Lobectomy,* history of, for a nontuberculous nonmalignant lesion with residual pulmonary disease. Removal of more than one lobe is cause for rejection regardless of the absence of residuals.

j. *Other traumatic lesions* of the chest or its contents.

★k. Pneumothorax or history thereof within 1 year of date of examination if due to simple trauma or surgery; within 3 years of date of examination if of spontaneous origin. Surgical correction is acceptable if no significant residual disease or deformity remains and pulmonary function tests are within normal limits.

2–12

l. Recent fracture of ribs, sternum, clavicle, or scapula.

m. Significant abnormal findings on physical examination of the chest.

2–25. Tuberculous Lesions
(See para 2–38.)
The causes for rejection for appointment, enlistment, and induction are—

a. Tuberculosis, active at any time within the past two years, in any form or location. A positive tuberculin skin test without other evidence of active disease is not disqualifying. Individuals taking prophylactic chemotherapy because of recent skin test conversion are not disqualified.

b. **Rescinded.**

c. Substantiated history of one or more reactivations or relapses of pulmonary tuberculosis, or other definite evidence of poor host resistance to the tubercle bacillus.

2–26. Nontuberculous Lesions
The causes for rejection for appointment, enlistment, and induction are—

a. Acute mastitis, chronic cystic mastitis, if more than mild.

b. Bronchial asthma, except for childhood asthma with a trustworthy history of freedom from symptoms since the 12th birthday.

c. Bronchitis, chronic with evidence of pulmonary function disturbance.

d. Bronchiectasis.

e. Bronchopleural fistula.

f. Bullous or generalized pulmonary emphysema.

g. Chronic abscess of lung.

h. Chronic fibrous pleuritis of sufficient extent to interfere with pulmonary function or obscure the lung field in the roentgenogram.

i. Chronic mycotic diseases of the lung including coccidioidomycosis; residual cavitation or more than a few small sized inactive and stable residual modules demonstrated to be due to mycotic disease.

j. Empyema, residual sacculation or unhealed sinuses of chest wall following operation for empyema.

k. Extensive pulmonary fibrosis from any cause, producing dyspnea on exertion.

l. Foreign body of the lung or mediastinum causing symptoms or active inflammatory reaction.

m. Multiple cystic disease of the lung or solitary cyst which is large and incapacitating.

n. New growth of breast; history of mastectomy.

o. Osteomyelitis of rib, sternum, clavicle, scapula, or vertebra.

p. Pleurisy with effusion of unknown origin within the previous 2 years.

q. Sarcoidosis. See paragraph 2–38.

r. Suppurative periostitis of rib, sternum, clavicle, scapula, or vertebra.

Section XIV. MOUTH, NOSE, PHARYNX, TRACHEA, ESOPHAGUS, AND LARYNX

2–27. Mouth
The causes for rejection for appointment, enlistment, and induction are—

a. Hard palate, perforation of.

b. Harelip, unless satisfactorily repaired by surgery.

c. Leukoplakia, if severe.

d. Lips, unsightly mutilations of, from wounds, burns, or disease.

e. Ranula, if extensive. For other tumors see paragraphs 2–10 and 2–41.

2–28. Nose
The causes for rejection for appointment, enlistment, and induction are—

a. Allergic manifestations.
   (1) Chronic atrophic rhinitis.

(2) Hay fever if severe; and if not controllable by antihistamines or by desensitization, or both.

b. *Choana, atresia, or stenosis* of, if symptomatic.

c. *Nasal septum,* perforation of:

★(1) Associated with the interference of function, ulceration or crusting, and when the result of organic disease.

(2) If progressive.

(3) If respiration is accompanied by a whistling sound.

d. *Sinusitis,* acute.

e. *Sinusitis,* chronic, when more than mild:

(1) Evidenced by any of the following: Chronic purulent nasal discharge, large nasal polyps, hyperplastic changes of the nasal tissues, or symptoms requiring frequent medical attention.

(2) Confirmed by transillumination or X-ray examination or both.

2–29. Pharynx, Trachea, Esophagus, and Larynx

The causes for rejection for appointment, enlistment, and induction are—

a. *Esophagus,* organic disease of, such as ulceration, varices, achalasia; peptic esophagitis; if confirmed by appropriate X-ray or esophagoscopic examinations.

b. *Laryngeal paralysis,* sensory or motor, due to any cause.

c. *Larynx,* organic disease of, such as neoplasm, polyps, granuloma, ulceration, and chronic laryngitis.

★d. *Plica dysphonia ventricularis.*

e. *Tracheostomy or tracheal fistula.*

2–30. Other Defects and Diseases

The causes for rejection for appointment, enlistment, and induction are—

a. *Aphonia.*

b. *Deformities or conditions of the mouth, throat, pharynx, larynx, esophagus, and nose* which interfere with mastication and swallowing of ordinary food, with speech, or with breathing.

c. *Destructive syphilitic disease of the mouth, nose, throat, larynx, or esophagus* (para 2–42)

d. *Pharyngitis and nasopharyngitis,* chronic, with postive history and objective evidence, if of such a degree as to result in excessive time lost in the military environment.

Section XV. NEUROLOGICAL DISORDERS

2–31. Neurological Disorders

The causes for rejection for appointment, enlistment, and induction are—

a. *Degenerative disorders.*

(1) Cerebellar and Friedreich's ataxia.

(2) Cerebral arteriosclerosis.

(3) Encephalomyelitis, residuals of, which preclude the satisfactory performance of military duty.

(4) Huntington's chorea.

(5) Multiple sclerosis.

(6) Muscular atrophies and dystrophies of any type.

b. *Miscellaneous.*

(1) Congenital malformations if associated with neurological manifestations and meningocele even if uncomplicated.

(2) Migraine when frequent and incapacitating.

(3) Paralysis or weakness, deformity, discoordination, pain, sensory disturbance, intellectual deficit, disturbances of consciousness, or personality abnormalities regardless of cause which is of such a nature or degree as to preclude the satisfactory performance of military duty.

(4) Tremors, spasmodic torticollis, athetosis or other abnormal movements more than mild.

c. *Neurosyphilis* of any form (general paresis, tabes dorsalis, meningovascular syphilis).

★d. *Paroxysmal convulsive disorders,* disturbances of consciousness, all forms of psychomotor or temporal lobe epilepsy or history thereof except for seizures associated with toxic states or fever during childhood up to the age of 5.

e. *Peripheral nerve disorder.*

(1) Polyneuritis.

(2) Mononeuritis or neuralgia which is chronic or recurrent and of an intensity that is periodically incapacitating.

(3) Neurofibromatosis.

f. *Spontaneous subarachnoid hemorrhage,* verified history of, unless cause has been surgically corrected.

Section XVI. PSYCHOSES, PSYCHONEUROSES, AND PERSONALITY DISORDERS

2–32. Psychoses

The causes for rejection for appointment, enlistment, and induction are—

Psychosis or authenticated history of a psychotic illness other than those of a brief duration associated with a toxic or infectious process.

2–33. Psychoneuroses

The causes for rejection for appointment, enlistment, and induction are—

a. *History of a psychoneurotic reaction* which caused—

(1) Hospitalization.

(2) Prolonged care by a physician.

(3) Loss of time from normal pursuits for repeated periods even if of brief duration, or

(4) Symptoms or behavior of a repeated nature which impaired school or work efficiency.

b. *History of a brief psychoneurotic reaction* or nervous disturbance within the preceding 12 months which was sufficiently severe to require medical attention or absence from work or school for a brief period (maximum of 7 days).

2–34. Personality Disorders

The causes for rejection for appointment, enlistment, and induction are—

a. *Character and behavior disorders,* as evidenced by—

(1) Frequent encounters with law enforcement agencies, or antisocial attitudes or behavior which, while not a cause for administrative rejection, are tangible evidence of an impaired characterological capacity to adapt to the military service.

(2) Overt homosexuality or other forms of sexual deviant practices such as exhibitionism, transvestism, voyeurism, etc.

(3) Chronic alcoholism or alcohol addiction.

(4) Drug addiction.

b. *Character and behavior disorders* where it is evident by history and objective examination that the degree of immaturity, instability, personality inadequacy, and dependency will seriously interfere with adjustment in the military service as demonstrated by repeated inability to maintain reasonable adjustment in school, with employers and fellow-workers, and other society groups.

c. *Other symptomatic immaturity reactions* such as authenticated evidence of enuresis which is habitual or persistent, not due to an organic condition (para 2-15c) occurring beyond early adolescence (age 12 to 14) and stammering or stuttering of such a degree that the individual is normally unable to express himself clearly or to repeat commands

d. *Specific learning defects* secondary to organic or functional mental disorders.

Section XVII. SKIN AND CELLULAR TISSUES

2–35. Skin and Cellular Tissues

The causes for rejection for appointment, enlistment, and induction are—

a. Acne. Severe, when the face is markedly disfigured, or when extensive involvement of the neck, shoulders, chest, or back would be aggravated by or interfere with the wearing of military equipment.

b. Atopic dermatitis. With active or residual lesions in characteristic areas (face and neck, antecubital and popliteal fossae, occasionally wrists and hands), or documented history thereof.

c. Cysts.

(1) *Cysts, other than pilonidal.* Of such a size or location as to interfere with the normal wearing of military equipment.

(2) *Cysts, pilonidal.* Pilonidal cysts, if evidenced by the presence of a tumor mass or a discharging sinus.

d. Dermatitis factitia.

e. Dermatitis herpetiformis.

f. Eczema. Any type which is chronic and resistant to treatment.

f.1 Elephantiasis or chronic lymphedema.

g. Epidermolysis bullosa; pemphigus.

h. Fungus infections, systemic or superficial types: If extensive and not amenable to treatment.

i. Furunculosis. Extensive, recurrent, or chronic.

j. Hyperhidrosis of hands or feet. Chronic or severe.

k. Ichthyosis. Severe.

l. Leprosy. Any type.

m. Leukemia cutis mycosis fungoides; Hodgkins' disease.

n. Lichen planus.

o. Lupus erythematosus (acute, subacute, or chronic) or any other dermatosis aggravated by sunlight.

p. Neurofibromatosis (Von Recklinghausen's disease).

q. Nevi or vascular tumors. If extensive, unsightly, or exposed to constant irritation.

r. Psoriasis or a verified history thereof.

s. Radiodermatitis.

t. Scars which are so extensive, deep, or adherent that they may interfere with the wearing of military equipment, or that show a tendency to ulcerate.

u. Scleroderma. Diffuse type.

v. Tuberculosis. See paragraph 2–38.

w. Urticaria. Chronic.

x. Warts, plantar, which have materially interfered with the following of a useful vocation in civilian life.

y. Xanthoma. If disabling or accompanied by hypercholesterolemia or hyperlipemia.

z. Any other chronic skin disorder of a degree or nature which requires frequent outpatient treatment or hospitalization, interferes with the satisfactory performance of duty, or is so disfiguring as to make the individual objectionable in ordinary social relationships.

★*aa.* When in the opinion of the examining physician tattoos will significantly limit effective performance of military service the individual will be referred to the AFEES Commander, for final determination of acceptability.

224

Section XVIII. SPINE, SCAPULAE, RIBS, AND SACROILIAC JOINTS

2–36. Spine and Sacroiliac Joints
(See also para 2–11.)

The causes for rejection for appointment, enlistment, and induction are—

a. Arthritis. See paragraph 2–11a.

★*b. Complaint of disease or injury of the spine or sacroiliac joints* either with or without objective signs which has prevented the individual from successfully following a physically active vocation in civilian life. Substantiation or documentation of the complaint without objective signs is required.

★*c. Deviation or curvature of spine* from normal alignment, structure, or function (scoliosis, kyphosis, or lordosis) if—

(1) Mobility and weight-bearing power is poor.

(2) More than moderate restriction of normal physical activities is required.

(3) Of such a nature as to prevent the individual from following a *physically active vocation* in civilian life.

(4) Of a degree which will interfere with the wearing of a uniform or military equipment.

★(5) Symptomatic associated with positive physical findings(s) and demonstrable by X-ray.

d. Diseases of the lumbosacral or sacroiliac joints of a chronic type and obviously associated with pain referred to the lower extremities, muscular spasm, postural deformities and limitation of motion in the lumbar region of the spine.

e. Granulomatous diseases either active or healed.

f. Healed fracture of the spine or pelvic bones with associated symptoms which have prevented the individual from following a *physically* active vocation in civilian life or which preclude the satisfactory performance of military duty.

g. Ruptured nucleus pulposus (herniation of intervertebral disk) or history of operation for this condition.

h. Spondylolysis or spondylolisthesis that is symptomatic or is likely to interfere with performance of duty or is likely to require assignment limitations.

2–37. Scapulae, Clavicles, and Ribs
(See para 2–11.)

The causes for rejection for appointment, enlistment, and induction are—

a. Fractures, until well-healed, and until determined that the residuals thereof will **not** preclude the satisfactory performance of military duty.

b. Injury within the preceding 6 **weeks,** without fracture, or dislocation, of more **than** a minor nature.

c. Osteomyelitis of rib, sternum, clavicle, scapula, or vertebra.

d. Prominent scapulae interfering with function or with the wearing of uniform or military equipment.

Section XIX. SYSTEMIC DISEASES AND MISCELLANEOUS CONDITIONS AND DEFECTS

2–38. Systemic Diseases

The causes for rejection for appointment, enlistment, and induction are—

a. Dermatomyositis.

b. Lupus erythematosus, acute, subacute, or chronic.

c. Progressive systemic sclerosis.

d. Reiter's disease.

e. Sarcoidosis.

f. Scleroderma, diffuse type.

g. Tuberculosis.

2–17

(1) Active tuberculosis in any form or location or substantiated history of active tuberculosis within the previous 2 years.

(2) Substantiated history of one or more reactivations or relapses of tuberculosis in any form or location or other definite evidence of poor host resistance to the tubercle bacillus.

(3) Residual physical or mental defects from past tuberculosis that would preclude the satisfactory performance of duty.

(4) (Deleted).

2-39. General and Miscellaneous Conditions and Defects

The causes for rejection for appointment, enlistment, and induction are—

a. Allergic manifestations.

(1) Allergic rhinitis (hay fever). See paragraph 2-28.

(2) Asthma. See paragraph 2-26b.

(3) Allergic dermatoses. See paragraph 2-35.

(4) Visceral, abdominal, and cerebral allergy, if severe or not responsive to treatment.

(5) Bona fide history of moderate or severe generalized (as opposed to local) allergic reaction to insect bites or stings. Bona fide history of severe generalized reaction to common foods, e.g., milk, eggs, beef, and pork.

b. Any acute pathological condition, including acute communicable diseases, until recovery has occurred without sequelae.

c. Any deformity which is markedly unsightly or which impairs general functional ability to such an extent as to prevent satisfactory performance of military duty.

d. Chronic metallic poisoning especially beryllium, manganese, and mercury. Undesirable residuals from lead, arsenic, or silver poisoning make the examinee medically unacceptable.

★e. Cold injury, residuals of (example: frostbite, chilblain, immersion foot, or trench foot), such as deep-seated ache, paresthesia, hyperhidrosis, easily traumatized skin, cyanosis, amputation of any digit, or ankylosis.

f. Positive tests for syphilis with negative TPI test unless there is a documented history of adequately-treated lues or any of the several conditions which are known to give a false-positive S.T.S. (vaccinia, infectious hepatitis, immunizations, atypical pneumonia, etc.) or unless there has been a reversal to a negative S.T.S. during an appropriate followup period (3 to 6 months).

g. Filariasis; trypanosomiasis; amebiasis; schistosomiasis; uncinariasis (hookworm) associated with anemia, malnutrition, etc., if more than mild, and other similar worm or animal parasitic infestations, including the carrier states thereof.

h. Heat pyrexia (heatstroke, sunstroke, etc.): Documented evidence of predisposition (includes disorders of sweat mechanism and previous serious episode), recurrent episodes requiring medical attention, or residual injury resulting therefrom (especially cardiac, cerebral, hepatic, and renal).

i. Industrial solvent and other chemical intoxication, chronic including carbon bisulfide, tricholorethylene, carbon tetrachloride, and methyl cellosolve.

j. Mycotic infection of internal organs.

k. Myositis or fibrositis; severe, chronic.

l. Residuals of tropical fevers and various parasitic or protozoal infestations which in the opinion of the medical examiner preclude the satisfactory performance of military duty.

Section XX. TUMORS AND MALIGNANT DISEASES

2-40. Benign Tumors

The causes for rejection for appointment, enlistment, and induction are—

a. Any tumor of the—

(1) Auditory canal, if obstructive.

(2) Eye or orbit, (para 2-12a(6)).

(3) Kidney, bladder, testicle, or penis.

(4) Central nervous system and its membraneous coverings unless 5 years after surgery and no otherwise disqualifying residuals of

226

surgery or of original lesion.

b. Benign tumors of the abdominal wall if sufficiently large to interfere with military duty.

c. Benign tumors of bone likely to continue to enlarge, be subjected to trauma during military service, or show malignant potential.

d. Benign tumors of the thyroid or other structures of the neck, including enlarged lymph nodes, if the enlargement is of such degree as to interfere with the wearing of a uniform or military equipment.

e. Tongue, benign tumor of, if it interferes with function.

f. Breast, thoracic contents, or chest wall, tumors, of, other than fibromata lipomata, and

inclusion or sebaceous cysts which do not interfere with military duty.

g. For tumors of the internal or external female genitalia see paragraph 2-14h.

2-41. Malignant Diseases and Tumors

The causes for rejection for appointment, enlistment, and induction are—

a. Leukemia, acute or chronic.

b. Malignant lymphomata.

★*c. Malignant tumor,* except for small early basal cell epitheliomas, at any time, even though surgically removed, confirmed by accepted laboratory procedures.

Section XXI. VENEREAL DISEASES

2-42. Venereal Diseases

In general the finding of acute, uncomplicated venereal disease which can be expected to respond to treatment is not a cause for medical rejection for military service. The causes for rejection for appointment, enlistment, and induction are—

a. Chronic venereal disease which has not satisfactorily responded to treatment. The finding of a positive serologic test for syphilis

following the adequate treatment of syphilis is not in itself considered evidence of chronic venereal disease which has not responded to treatment (para 2-39f).

b. Complications and permanent residuals of venereal disease if progressive, of such nature as to interfere with the satisfactory performance of duty, or if subject to aggravation by military service.

c. Neurosyphilis. See paragraph 2-31c.

★Section XXII. VOCATIONAL WAIVERS

(Rescinded)

★APPENDIX II

TABLES OF ACCEPTABLE AUDIOMETRIC HEARING LEVEL

Hearing of all applicants for appointment, enlistment, or induction will be tested by audiometers calibrated to either American Standards Association (ASA), or International Standards Organization (ISO) Standards.

All audiometric tracings or audiometric reading recorded on reports of medical examination or other medical records will be clearly identified "Results ASA–1951" or "Results ISO."

Table I. Acceptable Audiometric Hearing Level for Appointment, Enlistment and Induction

American Standards Association (ASA)		International Standards Organization (ISO)	
Cycles per second (hz)	Both ears	Cycles per second (hz)	Both ears
500 1000 2000	Average of the 6 readings (3 per ear) in the three speech frequencies not greater than twenty (20) decibels with no level greater than twenty-five (25) decibels.	500 1000 2000	Average of the 6 readings (3 per ear) in the speech frequencies not greater than thirty (30) decibels with no level greater than thirty-five (35).
4000	50 (each ear)	4000	55 (each ear)

OR

If the average of the three speech frequencies is greater than 20 decibels (ASA) or 30 decibels ISO reevaluate the better ear only in accordance with the following table of acceptability.

	ASA	ISO
500 (hz)	15 decibels	30 decibels
1000 (hz)	15 decibels	25 decibels
2000 (hz)	15 decibels	25 decibels
4000 (hz)	30 decibels	35 decibels

The poorer ear may be totally deaf.

A2–1

Table IV. Conversion Table. (To convert Individual Audiograms from the American Standards Association (ASA) to International Standards Organization (ISO))

AT	ADD
250 cps	15 db
500 cps	15 db
1000 cps	10 db
2000 cps	10 db
3000 cps	10 db
4000 cps	5 db
6000 cps	10 db
8000 cps	10 db

Identify the results of each audiogram as "ASA" or "ISO."

A2–3

228

APPENDIX III

TABLES OF WEIGHT

Table 1. Table of Militarily Acceptable Weight (in Pounds) as Related to Age and Height for Males—Initial Procurement

Height (inches)	Minimum (regardless of age)	Maximum					
		16–20 years	21–24 years	25–30 years	31–35 years	36–40 years	41 years and over
60	100	163	173	173	173	168	164
61	102	171	176	175	175	171	166
62	103	174	178	178	177	173	169
63	104	178	182	181	180	176	171
64	105	183	184	185	185	180	175
65	106	187	190	191	190	185	180
66	107	191	196	197	196	190	185
67	111	196	201	202	201	195	190
68	115	202	207	208	207	201	195
69	119	208	213	214	212	206	200
70	123	214	219	219	218	211	205
71	127	219	224	225	223	216	210
72	131	225	231	232	230	224	216
73	135	231	239	238	237	230	223
74	139	237	246	246	243	236	229
75	143	243	253	253	251	243	235
76	147	248	260	260	257	250	241
77	151	254	267	267	264	256	248
78	153	260	275	273	271	263	254
★*79	159	266	281	279	277	269	260
★*80	166	273	288	286	284	276	267

★*Applies only to personnel enlisted, inducted or appointed in Army and enlisted or inducted into Air Force. Does not apply to Navy or Marine Corps enlistees or inductees.

229

Change 28, effective June 14, 1972

Paragraph 7-12.   Dental--Induction, Enlistment, or Appointment
(see para. 2-5)

a. Except for physicians, dentists, and allied medical specialists, individuals who have orthodontic appliances and who are under active treatment are administratively unacceptable for enlistment or induction into the active or reserve components of the Army, Air Force, Navy and Marine Corps for an initial period not to exceed twelve months from the date that treatment was initiated. Selective Service registrants will be re-examined after the twelve-month period. After the twelve-month period, wherein a longer period of treatment is allegedly required, the registrant will be scheduled by the examining AFEES for consultation by a civilian or military orthodontist and a report of this consultation will be forwarded through the Chief, Medical Section, Headquarters, USAREC, Hampton, Virginia 23360 to HDQA (DASG-HES-P), Washington, D.C. 20314, for final determination of acceptability. The Surgeon General will coordinate, as appropriate, with the Surgeon General, United States Air Force, or the Chief, Bureau of Medicine and Surgery, Department of the Navy, on individuals whose induction into the Air Force, Navy or Marine Corps is being considered. Physicians, dentists, and allied medical specialists liable for induction will be evaluated in accord with the standards prescribed by Chapter 8 of the regulation.

****

e. Individuals with retainer orthodontic appliances who are not required to undergo active treatment are administratively acceptable for appointment, enlistment or induction.

230

D. FOOTNOTES

Abbreviations

Army Regulations = **AR**

President's Message to Congress on Selective Service Reform, February 12, 1980 = **President's Report**

Selective Service Law Reporter = **SSLR**

Selective Service Regulations = **Reg.**

Chapter 1:HOW THE DRAFT SYSTEM WORKS
1. 50 USC App. Sec. 451 et seq.
2. President's Report, p. 10
3. Reg. Sec. 1603.3
4. Reg. Sec. 1604.52
5. Reg. Sec. 1626.1
6. Reg. Sec. 1627.1
7. AR 601-270
8. Reg. Sec. 1622.44
9. Reg. Sec. 1626.2
10. President's Report, pp. 15-16
11. President's Report, p. 21
12. 50 USC App. Sec. 467(c)
13. Regs. Secs. 1622.1 - 1622.60

Chapter 2:
THE DRAFT LOTTERY
1. Reg. Sec. 1631.1
2. Reg. Sec. 1631.6(c)(2)
3. Reg. Sec. 1631.6(b)
4. Reg. Sec. 1631.6(d)(5)
5. Reg. Sec. 1631.6(d)(2)
6. Reg. Sec. 1631.6(b)(6)
7. Reg. Sec. 1631.6(d)(2)
8. Reg. Sec. 1631.6(d)(3)
9. Reg. Sec. 1631.6(d)(4)

Chapter 4: REGISTRATION AND RESISTANCE
1. 50 USC App. Sec. 463
2. President's Report, p. 10
3. President's Report, p. 9
4. 50 USC App. Sec. 462
5. 50 USC App. Sec. 462
6. Disposition of Defendants, 1944-1970, SSLR 6001-6005
7. 50 USC App. Sec. 462
8. 50 USC App. Sec. 462(d)
9. Reg. Sec. 1641.1(a)

Chapter 5:
CLASSIFICATION
1. President's Report, pp. 15-16
2. Ibid.
3. Reg. Sec. 1621.12
4. Reg. Sec. 1608.3(a)(1)
5. Ibid.
6. Ibid.
7. President's Report, pp. 15-16
8. Reg. Secs. 1621.11, 1621.12

9. Reg. Sec. 1625.14
10. Reg. Secs. 1622.1(a), 1623.1(b)
11. Reg. Sec. 1624.6
12. Reg. Sec. 1623.2

Chapter 6:
CONSCIENTIOUS OBJECTION
1. Clay v. US, 403 US 698 (1971)
2. Reg. Secs. 1660.2, 1660.4(a)
3. Reg. Sec. 1622.44
4. Reg. Sec. 1622.11
5. Reg. Sec. 1622.14
6. Reg. Sec. 1660.4
7. US v. Seeger, 380 US 163 (1965);
Welsh v. US, 398 US 333 (1970)
8. Clay v. US, supra.
9. Gilette v. US, 401 US 437 (1971)
10. Fleming v. US, 344 F.2d 912 (10th Cir. 1965)
11. Sicurella v. US, 348 US 385 (1955)
12. Reg. Sec. 1641.1
13. US v. Abbott, 425 F. 2d 910 (8th Cir. 1970)
14. Ehlert v. US, 402 US 99 (1971)
15. Reg. Sec. 1625.2
16. Reg. Sec. 1660.4(b)
17. Reg. Sec. 1660.4(a)
18. Gibson, Dodez v. US, 329 US 338 (1946); Reg. Sec. 1660.8
19. Reg. Sec. 1660.9(e)
20. Lockhart v. US, 420 F.2d 1143 (1969)
21. Reg. Sec. 1627.1
22. Reg. Sec. 1625.2
23. Disposition of Defendants, 1944-1970, SSLR 6001-6005
24. Ibid.

Chapter 7:
DEPENDENCY DEFERMENTS
1. Reg. Sec. 1622.30
2. Reg. Secs. 1622.30(a)(1)-(3)
3. Reg. Sec. 1622.30(a)(1)
4. Reg. Sec. 1622.30(c)
5. Reg. Sec. 1624.1(b)
6. Reg. Sec. 1624.3
7. Reg. Sec. 1622.30(b)

Chapter 8: SURVIVING SONS
1. McKart v. US, 395 US 185 (1969)
2. Reg. Sec. 1622.45
3. Public Law 92-129, Sec.101(d)(3)
4. McKart v. US, supra.
5. 50 USC App. Sec. 456(o)(1)
6. 50 USC App. Sec. 456(o)(2)
7. 50 USC App. Sec. 456(o)
8. McKart v. US, supra.

Chapter 9: MINISTERS
1. Reg. Sec. 1622.43
2. Reg. Sec. 1622.27
3. 50 USC App. Sec. 466(g)
4. 50 USC App. Sec. 466(g)(3)
5. Dickinson v. US, 346 US 389 (1953)
6. US v. Pryor, 488 F.2d 1273 (9th Cir. 1971)
7. 50 USC App. Sec. 466(g)
8. Reg. Sec. 1622.27

Chapter 10: MEDICAL SPECIALISTS AND STUDENTS
1. 50 USC App. Sec. 455(a), Reg. Secs. 1622.15, 1680 et seq.
2. Reg. Secs. 1680.1 - 1680.11
3. Reg. Sec. 1680.2
4. Reg. Secs. 1622.15, 1622.17, 1622.19, 1680.9
5. Reg. Sec. 1680.5(c)
6. Ibid.
7. Reg. Sec. 1680.5(b)(1)-(6)
8. Reg. Secs. 1680.3, 1680.6
9. Reg. Sec. 1680.5
10. Reg. Sec. 1622.28
11. Reg. Sec. 1680.9
12. AR 40-501, Chapter 8
13. Reg. Sec. 1622.26

Chapter 11: DISAGREEABLE CLASSIFICATION
1. Reg. Sec. 1624.1(a)
2. Reg. Secs. 1624.7, 1626.6, 1627.7
3. Reg. Sec. 1624.1(b)
4. Reg. Secs. 1624.1(b), 1626.2
5. Reg. Sec. 1626.2
6. Reg. Secs. 1641.1(a)
7. Reg. Sec. 1608.13(a)
8. Reg. Sec. 1608.22
9. Ibid.

Chapter 12: LOCAL BOARD PERSONAL APPEARANCE
1. Reg. Sec. 1624.1(a)
2. Reg. Sec. 1624.1(b)
3. Reg. Sec. 1623.4(c)
4. Reg. Sec. 1624.6
5. Reg. Sec. 1624.2
6. Reg. Sec. 1624.4(b)
7. Ibid.
8. Reg. Sec. 1624.4(e)
9. Reg. Sec. 1624.4(c)
10. Ibid.
11. Reg. Sec. 1624.44(a)
12. Reg. Sec. 1631.6(d)(5)
13. 50 USC App. Sec. 462(a)
14. Reg. Sec. 1623.4(c)
15. Reg. Sec. 1622.1(b)
16. Reg. Secs. 1661.6(a), (c)
17. US v. Hayden, 445 F.2d 1365 (9th Cir. 1971)
18. Reg. Sec. 1624.3
19. Reg. Sec. 1624.4(a)
20. Reg. Sec. 1604.52
21. Reg. Sec. 1624.4(b)
22. Reg. Sec. 1624.4(c)
23. Reg. Sec. 1626.2
24. Reg. Sec. 1626.4(c)
25. Reg. Sec. 1626.4(b)

Chapter 13: THE STATE APPEAL
1. Reg. Sec. 1626.2
2. Reg. Sec. 1626.4(b)
3. Reg. Sec. 1626.3(c)
4. Reg. Sec. 1626.4(b)
5. Reg. Sec. 1624.6
6. Reg. Sec. 1608.13(a)
7. Reg. Sec. 1608.22
8. Reg. Sec. 1626.2
9. Reg. Sec. 1626.4(c)
10. Ibid.
11. Reg. Sec. 1627.1(b)
12. Reg. Sec. 1627.3(e)
13. Reg. Sec. 1627.1(a)
14. Reg. Sec. 1626.1

15. Reg. Sec. 1625.2(a)
16. Ibid.

Chapter 14:
THE MEDICAL EXAMINATION
1. Reg. Sec. 1622.44
2. Reg. Sec. 1622.44(a), AR 601-270, Chapter 3, Par. 3-31
3. AR 40-501, Chapters 2, 6, 8
4. Reg. Sec. 1622.44(a)
5. AR 40-501, Chapter 1, Par. 1-2(a)
6. AR 601-270, Chapter 4, Par. 4-10
7. AR 601-270, Chapter 3, Par. 3-31
8. US v. Anderson, 5 SSLR 3843 (9th Cir. 1972)
9. AR 40-501, Chapter 2, Par. 2-34(a)(2)
10. 50 USC App. Sec. 462 (a)
11. 50 USC App. Sec. 462 (a)

Chapter 15: INDUCTION
1. Department of Defense Directive 1300.6
2. President's Report, p. 16
3. Reg. Sec. 1632.2
4. Reg. Sec. 1622.44(a)
5. President's Report, p. 16
6. 50 USC App. Sec. 456(i); Reg. Sec. 1632.2(c)
7. Reg. Sec. 1631.6(a)
8. Reg. Secs. 1624.7, 1626.6, 1627.7
9. Reg. Sec. 1632.1(a)
10. Reg. Sec. 1631.6(b)
11. Reg. Secs. 1625.2(a), 1625.14

12. Reg. Sec. 1632.2(a)
13. Reg. Sec. 1632.2(b)
14. Reg. Sec. 1625.2(a)
15. Ehlert v. US, 402 US 99 (1971)
16. Reg. Sec. 1632.10
17. Reg. Sec. 1632.20
18. Disposition of Defendants, 1944-1970, SSLR 6001-6005
19. Ibid.

Chapter 16:
DRAFT CASES IN COURT
1. 50 USC App. Sec. 460(b)(3)
2. 50 USC App. Sec. 462(a)
3. Dickinson v. US, 346 US 389 (1953)
4. Reg. Secs. 1624.6, 1626.4(i), 1627.4(h)
5. US v. Haughton, 413 F.2d 736 (9th Cir. 1969)
6. US v. Hayden, 445 F.2d 1365 (9th Cir. 1971)
7. Ibid.
8. US v. Andersen, 447 F.2d 1063 (9th Cir. 1971)
9. US v. Atherton, 430 F.2d 741 (9th Cir. 1970)
10. Falbo v. US, 320 US 549 (1944)
11. For example: Arver v. US, 245 US 366 (1918); US v. Thomason, 444 F.2d 1094 (9th Cir. 1971); US v. Zaugh, 445 F.2d 300 (9th Cir. 1971); US v. Burns, 446 F.2d 896 (9th Cir. 1971); US v. Lumsden, 449 F.2d 154 (9th Cir. 1971)

12. Disposition of Defendants, 1944-1970, SSLR 6019
13. Ibid.
14. Ibid.
15. 18 USC Secs. 5005 et. seq.

Appendix A:
ALIENS AND THE DRAFT
1. 50 USC App. Secs. 453, 456(a)
2. 50 USC App. Sec. 453
3. Reg. Sec. 1641.1
4. 50 USC App. Sec. 455(a)(3)
5. Opinions of the Attorney General 28, April, 1968
6. Itzcovitz v. SS Board No. 6, 2 SSLR 3255 (SD-NY May 7, 1969)
7. Reg. Sec. 1622.42(e)
8. Reg. Sec. 1622.40(a)(3)
9. Reg. Sec. 1622.42(c)
10. Immig. & Nat. Act, Secs. 241(a)(1), 212(a)(22)
11. 50 USC App. Sec. 454(j)
12. AR 601-270, Par. 3-12(a), 3-9(c)
13. Trop v. Dulles, 345 US 86

235

THE LIVING TOGETHER KIT: This book is the all new, complete guide to living together. It shows the unmarried couple how to own property, deal with leases, insurance, credit, wills, custody and legitimacy of children, and dividing things when it's time to move on. Complete with tear-out fill-in contracts which cover different lifestyles, and a living together certificate. $8.95.

HOW TO CHANGE YOUR NAME (in California): Changing your name is cheap and easy. This book comes complete with all the legal forms you need to do it yourself. Full information on women's name problems, with special attention to women who want to retain their own names after marriage or return to them after divorce. $7.95.

HOW TO ADOPT YOUR STEPCHILD: Shows how to prepare the necessary legal forms and make your appearance in court. Also has information on how to get the consent of the natural parent, conduct an "abandonment" proceeding, change birth certificates. Private and agency adoptions are not covered. $10.00.

═══════════ BOOKS DISTRIBUTED BY NOLO PRESS ═══════════

IMMIGRATING TO THE U.S.A. (2nd ed.): The most comprehensive book available for the non-lawyer who is interested in immigration. Covers all aspects of immigration: student visas, work permits, preference categories, requirements for U.S. citizenship, non-immigrant visas, deportation laws, etc. Includes forms. $7.95.

LANDLORDING, By Leigh Robinson, Express: A practical guide for the conscientious landlord or landlady. Covers repairs, maintenance, getting good tenants, legal forms for doing your own evictions, record keeping and taxes. This is a large book, covering a many-sided subject. Even includes some basic carpentry. $12.50.

SMALL-TIME OPERATOR, By Bernard Kamoroff, Bell Springs Publishing: A guide to help you set up the "business" end of your business, and keep it lubricated and well maintained. It also serves as a workbook, and includes bookkeeping instructions and a complete set of ledgers. Information on permits, licenses, financing, loans, insurance, bank accounts, taxes, etc. $6.95.

ORDER FROM:

NOLO PRESS, Box 544, Occidental, CA 95465

or: 950 Parker St., Berkeley, CA 94710

Make your check or money order payable to Nolo Press. Please add 6% sales tax if you are ordering in California, and 75 cents postage and handling for each book.

THE NOLO PRESS LINE

OF "DO-IT-YOURSELF"

LAW BOOKS

CALIFORNIA TENANTS' HANDBOOK (5th ed.): Sound practical advice on getting deposits back, breaking a lease, getting repairs made, using Small Claims Court, dealing with the obnoxious landlord and forming a tenants' union. Contains numerous sample letters and agreements as well as a "fair-to-tenants" tear out lease and rental agreement. ". . . sharper than a serpent's tooth" — Herb Caen, S.F. Chronicle. $5.95.

PLANNING YOUR ESTATE: Brand new! Comprehensive information on making your own will, alternatives to probate, planning your own funeral, providing for your children, and lots of inheritance and estate tax tips. Information we all need, presented for the first time in words we can understand. $15.00.

PROTECT YOUR HOME WITH A DECLARATION OF HOMESTEAD (3rd ed.): Your house can be protected from creditors for up to $40,000 under California law only if you file a homestead. Here we tell you how to do it cheaply, easily and legally. An invaluable gift for the new homeowner. $4.95.

PEOPLE'S GUIDE TO CALIFORNIA MARRIAGE LAW (3rd ed.): Vital information on community and separate property, names, children of former marriages, buying a house, avoiding probate, etc. Includes a sample will and sample marriage contracts. A very detailed guide for problems as immediate as a child in trouble with the law, and as long-range as what to consider when buying a house. $6.95.

HOW TO COLLECT YOUR CHILD SUPPORT & ALIMONY: Step-by-step instructions on how to collect all that back support. Includes sections on how to find people and their property, as well as what to do when you do find them. This is one of the most valuable books we have ever published. $7.95.

CALIFORNIA DEBTORS' HANDBOOK (Formerly "How to Beat the Bill Collector"): A constructive guide for those who find themselves over their heads in legal debts. Contains information on wage attachments, child support debts, student loans, car repossessions, bankruptcy, etc. Also detailed information on how to deal with collection agencies. $5.95.

← more

**HOW TO FORM YOUR OWN CALIFORNIA CORPORA-
TION (3rd ed.):** All the forms and instructions necessary to
file your own California (profit) corporation. Includes information on limited liability and tax aspects of incorporating. Written for the 1977 simplified corporation laws, and updated for
1979. Includes tear-out by-laws, articles, minutes and fancy
stock certificates. $12.00.

**HOW TO BUILD A BIGGER AND BETTER HYDRO-
PONIC GARDEN for less than $20.** This one tells exactly
how to set up and operate the best, cheapest, easiest, most
fun and most productive small garden in captivity. Hand
printed. $3.95.

**THE CALIFORNIA NON-PROFIT CORPORATION
BOOK (2nd ed.):** This one will be available about March,
1980. It contains all the articles and by-laws necessary for
you to form your own non-profit corporation. Federal and state
tax and tax exemption is discussed in detail. $15.00.

OTHER BOOKS PUBLISHED

BY NOLO PRESS

HOW TO DO YOUR OWN DIVORCE IN CALIFORNIA (Seventh Edition): This famous
book revolutionized the divorce field by making it clear and simple to the
layperson. Tells you the practical things you need to think about and gives
information and advice on making your various decisions. Shows exactly
how to do your own. Over 200,000 copies in print have saved Californians
more than $15 million in attorney fees. New edition includes 1979 law
changes. (California only) $8.95

**EVERYBODY'S GUIDE TO SMALL CLAIMS COURT
(2nd ed.):** Small Claims Court jurisdiction is now $750 in
California, but we expect that with increasing consumer
pressure it will soon be lifted to $2,000. This book is a step-
by-step guide telling you how to evaluate your case, prepare
evidence and witnesses, how to present your case in court,
and how to collect your money when you win. $5.95.

HYDRO-STORY: The complete manual of hydroponic
gardening at home. All the basic information about this easy
and rewarding way to garden. Garden plans, greenhouse
designs, plantfood recipes, fantasies, and lots of photos and
drawings. $4.95

THE NOLO PRESS LINE
OF "DO-IT-YOURSELF"
LAW BOOKS